droppin'
science

straight-up talk from HIP HOP'S greatest voices

droppin'
science

straight-up talk from HIP HOP'S greatest voices

selected and edited by
DENISE L. McIVER

THREE RIVERS PRESS • NEW YORK

Grateful acknowledgment is made to the following for permission to reprint
previously published material:

Quotes taken from THE BOOTH (www.icast.com). Courtesy of icast.com.

Excerpts from "Has He No Shame" by Robert Hilburn, published May 14, 2000.
    Used by permission of the Los Angeles Times Syndicate.

Excerpts as published in *The Source*. Used by permission of The Source Publishing Inc.

"Pop's Rap III (All My Children)": Words and music by Rashid Lonnie Lynn and Rashid
    Lonnie Lynn Sr. © Copyright 2000 Songs of Universal, Inc., o/b/o itself, and
    Senseless Music, Inc. (BMI). International Copyright Secured. All Rights Reserved.

Quote from "Healthy, Wealthy, and Wise," June/July 2000. Used by permission of
    Vanguarde Media's *Honey* magazine.

Published by Three Rivers Press, New York, New York.
Member of the Crown Publishing Group, a division of Random House, Inc.
www.randomhouse.com

THREE RIVERS PRESS and the Tugboat design are registered trademarks of
Random House, Inc.

Printed in the United States of America

Design by Paula Kelly

Library of Congress Cataloging-in-Publication Data
    Droppin' science : straight-up talk from hip hop's greatest voices /
[collected by] Denise L. McIver.
    1. Conduct of life—Quotations, maxims, etc. 2. Quotations. I. Title:
Dropping science. II. McIver, Denise L.
PN6084 C556 D76   2002
081—dc21   2001040989

ISBN 0-609-80729-3

10 9 8 7 6 5 4 3 2 1

First Edition

THIS BOOK IS LOVINGLY DEDICATED

TO MICHAEL CROSBY, WHO SHOWED

ME A WORLD I HAVE COME TO LOVE.

CONTENTS

FOREWORD

To Our Brothers and Sisters:

You've seen our Break Dancin'. You've seen our Graffiti Art. You've heard our language and unique styles of music. You've seen our clothing trends. However, you still do not fully know who or what we are.

You may ask yourself, Why do I need to know who or what you are? The answer lies in whether you are interested in a strategy that relives human suffering, creates dialogue between races, and enhances your self-worth.

We are Hip Hop and we feel that a strategy like ours is good for the whole of society and should be shared by all. We are not forcing our view of the world on anyone; we are simply making our wonderful inner-city discovery, Hip Hop, known and available.

The freedom to inquire into the deeper meanings of Hip Hop, beyond Rap music, is yours. Those who wish to limit Hip Hop to music and dance are misleading themselves about the magnitude of our collective consciousness. We are proud to have discovered Hip Hop, and we are appreciative of our discovery because we are benefiting from its existence. Hip Hop has enhanced our health, love, awareness, and wealth—we can see no other contribution greater to the children of the inner city than Hip Hop.

Know this: Hip Hop is not Rap music. Hip Hop is an alternative behavior capable of transforming subjects and objects in an attempt to describe one's true character. Hip Hop, in its early days, was a direct response to the social indoctrination of the seventies' educational curriculum. Early Hip Hoppas demanded the freedom to see the world through their own eyes, not through the eyes of their predetermined education. Early Hip Hoppas developed a way to view the real world by discovering that everything was always something else: that the label given to a thing did not actually describe the existence of that thing. We discovered that people, places, and things, in their true essence, were nameless and that we had the authority to rename and redefine the world around us according to our true personalities. Not the personalities taught to us in grade school. For early Hip Hoppas in the mid-seventies, labels, titles, and names limited the possibilities of what people, places, and things could be. Once this was realized, early Hip Hoppas began to see themselves not as Larry, Pamela, David, Joe, or Mary, but as L-Boogie, Sweet-P, Disco-D, Fat Joe, or M-ski, which gave them new powers far beyond the average inner-city person's. Joseph Saddler changed his name to Grandmaster Flash and developed the power to create the mixer, which made it possible to transform the turntable from an appliance to an instrument. This was, is, and shall always be . . . Hip Hop. When Hip Hop expresses itself, it creates elements that help others to identify with it. These elements have been traditionally called Breakin', Emceein', Graffiti Art, DeeJayin', Beatboxin', Street Fashion, Street Language, Street Knowledge, and Street Entrepreneurialism. These elements, when expressed, create Hip Hop Kulture. Hip Hop Kulture is not Rap music. As you can see, Emceein', which is the correct term for what is commonly called Rapping, is but one element in a list of nine. Rap or Emceein' comes from Hip Hop. Hip Hop does not come from Rap.

Knowing this puts you in touch with a strategy that can be applied to any subject or object. Everything is always something else. If Hip Hop teaches us one thing, it is never to settle for appearances, titles, labels, or names. They are illusions that trap the mind. Hip Hop is a lifestyle or, rather, a style of life. A way to be. An attitude. A character. It is the name of our unique inner-city consciousness. It is invisible, indestructible, and free. It is not a thing that you can touch with hands or see with eyes. It is our blessing, a Divine way out, our strategy against sickness, hate, ignorance, and poverty. This was, is, and shall always be . . . Hip Hop!

This book is Hip Hop. It is designed to unconditionally open your heart and free your mind past limitations of fear and doubt. Why this book isn't in the philosophy, sociology, or even self-help section of your favorite bookstore should give you some idea as to how far we (Hip Hop) have to go before truly being intellectually respected. However, here lies the beauty of this book. For it represents the unpopular survival ideas found in the minds of a forgotten sect of American society. A sect of society whose whole generation was branded with an "X" and almost totally forgotten about . . . until now.

Not all of us died in the streets. Some of us mastered the streets and discovered a strategy capable of maintaining an even higher level of Inner-City existence. For some, this book is the beginning of a new awareness. For others, it is the confirmation of an awareness already expressed. Sort of a reminder. In any event, this book represents the accumulated wisdom of Inner-City "families." A life guide from the children of the ghetto.

Enjoy,

KRS-ONE *(aka "The Teacher")*

INTRODUCTION

I came to give praise and honor
And to identify my children who have been
sayin' and doin' the right things . . .

"Pop's Rap III (All My Children)"
from "LIKE WATER FOR CHOCOLATE"

Okay . . . are you ready?

I'm going to admit it. I'm addicted to wisdom.

As early as I can remember, it seems I've always had a lifelong thirst for wisdom. I think it began with *Aesop's Fables,* which my father would read and reread to my brother and me so that we would settle down long enough to fall asleep. I never tired of those stories, and with each retelling or rereading, I always learned something new, something that I had perhaps missed earlier— something that made the story all the richer and more real and meaningful.

Music, perhaps more than any other art form, can provide us with heartfelt wisdom. No one can deny the wisdom offered by something like Marvin Gaye's plaintive and prayerful "Wholy Holy," or his righteously angry "Inner City Blues (Make Me Wanna Holler)," or Grandmaster Flash & the Furious Five's "The Message." Not only does music make you *feel,* sometimes it can also make you *think.*

The book you now hold is a source of wisdom. What makes it different from others is that it looks to Hip Hop, and to the artists who create it. This book is for *you* . . . because as Pharoahe Monch said recently in an interview: "Hip Hop is an important tool. It's the voice of the people."

I wanted to honor and highlight the wisdom of today's Hip Hop artists. I realized that on a level playing field, they are not that much different from you and me. And just like you and me, many of these Hip Hop artists have had their share of hardships, disappointments, and letdowns. They've had to battle the streets, "playa hatas," and sometimes even their families (not to mention record-company executives). Many, like Eminem, were crust-bread poor and couldn't even afford diapers for their children; some, like Jay-Z, resorted to

11

slanging on the streets, then ended up selling millions of albums retelling his story of the "Hard Knock Life." Several of them grew up without a father, and many of them are parents themselves. Still, despite the difficulties, setbacks, and mistakes, something deep within enabled them to become success stories, despite the obstacles strewn in their path and the hurdles they've had to clear.

The wisdom of the artists represented in this book is real, profound, and honest. Some of their wisdom will make you laugh, but hopefully it will make you *think*. The artists represented here get it, and have been there themselves. Maybe that's <u>why</u> you're such a fan of their music. Life in the rap game is more than "bling-bling." Hard work and a belief in vision mixed with luck is what made these artists who they are today.

I am pleased and enormously grateful that "The Teacher," KRS-One (Knowledge Rules Supreme Over Nearly Everybody), enthusiastically agreed to write the foreword. It was his landmark 1987 recording, *Criminal Minded,* that set the stage for future like-minded conscious rappers and opened doors for folks like Common, Bahamadia, and Dead Prez.

The beauty of wisdom is that it is universal. So, whether you're a b-boy in the Inner City or a suburban teen in the middle of America, there's something for you to relate to and own. The artists in *Droppin' Science: Straight-up Talk from Hip Hop's Greatest Voices* demonstrate that no matter what you may be going through, yes, you can overcome and live successfully and even wisely.

This is my personal invitation to you to think, grow, and, hopefully, learn from these artists. Let their words of advice steep in your soul.

So c'mon. Let's do this!

Peace . . .

With affection,

DENISE L. McIVER
January 2002

OLD SCHOOL

Wisdom is the principal thing; therefore get wisdom: and with all thy getting get understanding.

PROVERBS 4:7

MIDDLE SCHOOL

A man is born with all the wisdom he needs for life.

DICK GREGORY

NEW SCHOOL

A clown can't imitate the wise, but the wise can imitate the clown.

DRAMA

Your potential is infinite
Be wise; visualize;
witness it . . .

GURU, "KEEP YOUR WORRIES,"
JAZZMATAZZ—STREETSOUL (VOL. 3)

Everybody gotta struggle, that's the way
   of the world,
Can't develop biceps if you don't do curls . . .

BLACKALICIOUS,
"MAKING PROGRESS," *NIA*

All the hardships that my family and I went through growing up made me the man I am today.

DORACELL

I definitely feel like I came a long way from where I was before, because I was a savage. [What changed me] was wanting to learn, wanting to be somebody. Just knowing what my gift is and wanting to carry that out.

MARY J. BLIGE

I was the class clown growing up. I did things the hard way. I wanted to do what I pleased. But I went through a lot of sh*t that changed my bad to good.

RED HANDED OF 1 LIFE 2 LIVE

You either learn from your experiences or go back and do the same thing, and I learned from my experiences.

MARY J. BLIGE

To reform me is to change me. But you can't change me because that means you'd have to change the experience that made me.

TRICK DADDY

You can't bathe in yesteryear's glory all the time. You gotta keep going and live your life.

Q-TIP

I done experienced certain things, and I ain't thinking like no shorty. I ain't livin' that life of gettin' blunted all day and night and not going to school or none of that sh*t.

COMMON

Change is a part of evolution.

BIG GIPP OF GOODIE MOB

I look at life and know that every moment that I go through is supposed to be there. I gotta appreciate the struggles and the good times, utilize the struggles to grow and create. . . . I wouldn't be here if it wasn't for my mistakes.

COMMON

When you stop growing, you die. Anything that's not growing is dead. Growth is essential for life and the only way to reach full maturation.

KHUJO OF GOODIE MOB

I never try to label what I do and categorize it, because I'm unlimited with whatever I do. I'm constantly growing as an individual.

COMMON

The present is a product of the past. If you're living for now, today—without any relationship or respect for what happened yesterday—you put yourself at risk of repeating the same mistake.

MOS DEF

I literally didn't have sh*t. So when I hit twenty-three, that was like a wake-up point for me. Like "I gotta do something now."

EMINEM

droppin' science

We are not afraid of growth; it's ain't no bad thing. It's like expanding a house—the front room stays the same, everything else just gets bigger and better.

JUICY J OF THREE 6 MAFIA

Even if you make a mistake, you learn and grow.

JAY-Z

I had to teach myself to be a man.

STICKY FINGAZ

You're used to doing something a certain way: you're used to hearing the music a certain way, you're used to moving, dressing, walking, talking a certain way. But when you're trying to tap in to something new, I know doing the same thing ain't gonna get it.

DRE OF OUTKAST

You're mad when you're young because you don't understand what the hell is going on, how things work, and what's expected of you. But once you understand that, you channel your energy to other places instead of just being pissed off, because you understand that that gets you nowhere.

ICE CUBE

I'm happy that I went through the struggle that I went through. I can't be ashamed of my personal life. . . . My personal life has made me stronger.

QUEEN PEN

ON SELF-ESTEEM AND BELIEVING IN YOURSELF 2

Don't let anybody tell you
What to hope and to fear . . .

DMX, "NO LOVE 4 ME,"
*FLESH OF MY FLESH, BLOOD
OF MY BLOOD*

I'm not always confident, but some days I feel like I can't be touched. And it's not about the clothes I wear. It's all about attitude.

EVE

My number-one insecurity is being a dark female. Back in the day, it was not the cool thing. That was just something I had to get over, because for a while I couldn't stand myself.

FOXY BROWN

It's hard to make the statement that being me is enough.

BAHAMADIA

Follow your heart and what you believe. Like I always say, persistence overcomes resistance. . . . As long as you believe, you can make a thousand people believe."

THIRSTIN HOWL III

When you feel good about yourself, you can do whatever you want to do.

MASTER P, CEO OF NO LIMIT RECORDS

I'm a tomboy. I'm comfortable every day, and I love myself. What's wrong with that?

DA BRAT

Only thing I could tell you [about being successful], you gotta believe in yourself. If you don't believe in yourself, you ain't gonna ever get nowhere. . . . I always had confidence in myself. If you believe in yourself, you can do whatever.

MASTER P, CEO OF NO LIMIT RECORDS

People can't make you unhappy unless you allow them to do that. I realized that I can't look for nobody else to make me happy.

MASE

I just do me and I believe in my sh*t.

SHYNE

The strong survive. If you stay with it and it's something you believe in, it's gonna pay off in the end. . . . Keep faith and you'll come back up.

LIL' TROY

My whole thing is, I took it one step at a time and believed in myself, believed in my company, and just kept working at it every day until the doors opened up. It's gonna be there when it's your time.

MASTER P, CEO OF NO LIMIT RECORDS

Me, personally, I don't get into labels. I can do whatever.

COMMON

I wanted to be like *me*, you know? I knew I had a talent like any other individual.

RAEKWON "THE CHEF" OF WU-TANG CLAN

I'm so secure in what I do that I don't care what anybody else is doing.

JAY-Z

ON SELF-ESTEEM AND BELIEVING IN YOURSELF

droppin' science

You can do anything if you set your mind to it and that's what you wanna do.

EMINEM

Honestly, if you stick to what you do, believe in it, then other people will believe in it. I believe in what I do, it's that simple. That's the bottom line, period.

RASCO OF CALI AGENTS
(March 30, 2000. *Rebirth* magazine: www.rebirthmag.com)

Beauty comes from the inside. If you don't love yourself or feel happy with who you are, your beauty will never show on the outside.

MARY J. BLIGE

Confidence is faith. If you can see it, you can believe it. . . . Arrogance is when you love yourself but you don't care about other people. . . . Confidence is when you can confidently walk around and believe, "Yo, I can do anything I put my mind to."

LL COOL J

Too many people aren't comfortable with themselves or look for what's wrong with other people rather than enhancing what's right about themselves. I think people need to focus more on utilizing what they have instead of killing themselves trying to fight their shortcomings.

RAH DIGGA

ON TRUTH 3

Curse to the wicked snakes who try to snatch
the truth away . . .

WU-TANG CLAN "JAH WORLD," *THE W*

droppin' science

People don't believe that white people are poor, they think that white people just got it made. I was the brokest motherf*cker on my block.

EMINEM

Happiness means appreciating everything I've been blessed with.

SEAN "P. DIDDY" COMBS

Everybody wants to hear the truth, but they're not ready.

FREDDIE FOXXX

You gotta be able to face the truth of who you are. If you are not able to face that truth of who you are, you're gonna crumble, man.

EVERLAST

The understanding that the truth gives you, and the freedom that the truth gives your heart, is something I think every man is capable of having and entitled to have.

RZA OF WU-TANG CLAN

People respect you a lot more when you keep it real.

KIMA OF TOTAL

If it ain't the truth, it ain't right.

BIG GIPP OF GOODIE MOB

Just give me the pure, raw honesty, y'know. I don't have time to be beating around the bush to appease people. Just tell the truth in a respectful way. That's what I try to do.

COMMON

If we can't tell the whole truth, let's not tell anything.

BIZZY BONE OF BONE THUGS-N-HARMONY

ON PASSION

4

She the one that make my life
feel complete,
'Cause I be like the lyric and
she be the beat . . .

**BLACK EYED PEAS,
"COMPLETE BELOVED,"**
LOVE & BASKETBALL

droppin' science

You should do it for the passion. Passion rules everything.

HEAVY D

Don't do anything you're not feeling.

TALIB KWELI OF BLACK STAR

When you hear the moniker "Genius," people expect you to be souped and hyper. But that's in all of us. It just depends on how you bring it out.

GZA "THE GENIUS" OF WU-TANG CLAN

Follow your heart.

RAH DIGGA

If you're scared to make what you feel, you shouldn't be making it at all.

HAVOC OF MOBB DEEP

When you start forgetting why you do what you do, you done off.

MR. CHEEKS OF THE LOST BOYZ

If you're passionate, people can't help but believe in it. The biggest lesson that I've learned is to do it from your heart. Let your heart speak. Be passionate, because people gravitate toward the truth.

Q-TIP

Whatever you do, yo, bang out! You got something you gotta do, bang out doin' it. 'Cause I did it. I've been through it and I'm still here. No matter what you got, no matter what you don't got, you still living—you good.

PUERTO ROCK

You can do anything you want to do, just make sure it's from the heart.

DJ U-NEEK

It may be the music, film, clothing, or whatever. I'm driven just to be the best at it. I'm trying to operate on the highest level I can.

JAY-Z

If you gonna do anything at all, do it. If you gonna push it, push it.

DRE OF OUTKAST

ON POWER AND RESPECT 5

First should always come respect . . .

KRS-ONE, "LIKE A THROTTLE,"
SEX AND VIOLENCE

Sometimes your sunshine get snatched
    like a necklace,
When you get too drunk on power and
    your drive gets reckless . . .

TALIB KWELI, "KNOW THAT,"
BLACK ON BOTH SIDES

Power is knowledge, but the manifestation of it is how you can change your environment. Power is the ability to change the things and the people around you, to move them in the direction that makes sense to you and the things around you.

RUSSELL SIMMONS, CEO OF DEF JAM RECORDS

You gotta be able to respect every man for what they do.

MASTER P, CEO OF NO LIMIT RECORDS

If you want the credit, do the work. That's the only way you can get respect.

PETE ROCK

It is strength, it's wisdom, and it is a form of intelligence. The smarter you get, the stronger you get, the more powerful you are. Power is a way of controlling your destination.

MASTER P, CEO OF NO LIMIT RECORDS

As a person, I'm open and giving. I give people a chance.

MR. SERV-ON

These young females need to know that they have to conduct themselves as women at all times. Don't expose what don't need to be exposed.

SNOOP DOGG

Do what you gotta do, and people are gonna respect you regardless.

RAEKWON OF WU-TANG CLAN

The people that respect you, respect you.

MOS DEF

A lot of times people have their own agendas, and you accept that people have got faults, and you've got to find your way through it and accept that you're not better than that person and that person is not better than you.

POSDNOUS OF DE LA SOUL

Your body is a tool God gave you.

WYCLEF JEAN

My whole message is big. I'm not here to be a preacher or nothing. But when you have a power, you can make some changes. . . . So your voice can change things. You can stop a lot of stuff.

ERICK SERMON

Strength has to come from the inside.

EVE

I believe that women can be just as strong as men if they put they mind to it.

LIL' KIM

Respect yourself. Don't give all of you away so easily.

JILL SCOTT

I believe, for a woman, respect should always matter. It should be first in your book. It was pounded into your head from day one, and you should always keep it in your mind and your heart. Respect is everything.

BIANCA OF MAJOR FIGGAS

ON FRIENDSHIP 6

Keep it real on the street,
    money,
And look out for one
    another . . .

KOOL G RAP, "FOR
DA BROTHAZ," 4, 5, 6

It's good to be around people that have the same goals.

TECH

You can always make more money. Once people are gone or locked up, there's no bringing back or finding lost time. Some cats just think about the money, but it's really about people and relationships.

JAY-Z

Watch who your friends are.

PRODIGY OF MOBB DEEP

Friendship is a spiritual bond. It is unconditional love, trust, honesty, loyalty, and truth; but most importantly, friendship is being oneself.

LIL' KIM

The same friends I had back then are the same people on tour with me now.

EMINEM

A loyal muthaf*cker is a n*gga who appreciate, who don't forget what somebody'll do for them.

REDMAN OF WU-TANG CLAN

Friendships are based on trust and sticking together in the spiritual sense.

MARY J. BLIGE

Friendship to me means loyalty, honesty, and trust. A friend is not only someone you can call in times of need but also when you're just looking to laugh and have a good time.

MISSY "MISDEMEANOR" ELLIOTT

Don't never sh*t on your n*ggas. Always keep it tight, because more minds is better than one.

DRAG-ON

People go through ups and downs, and if you're a real friend, you're gonna be there through the ups and downs . . .

LIL' KIM

If you claim to be down with people and you rolling with them, be loyal and ride with them . . . until there's nothing left to ride for.

BUSTA RHYMES

I keep my little circle of family and friends. . . . That's why I keep those friends around, because I know that those are the people that really care about me for me.

EMINEM

I only have a few friends, and I love them because they're honest and loyal and they tell me the truth.

DA BRAT

ON LOVE AND SEX 7

See I wanna get to know you so I
    can show you,
What a strong relationship can
    grow to . . .

**ERIC B. & RAKIM, "WHAT'S
ON YOUR MIND?"** *DON'T
SWEAT THE TECHNIQUE*

It ain't love when the motherf*ckin'
    sex cost money . . .

504 BOYZ, "CHECK 'EM,"
GOODFELLAS

Love is everything in my book. It's like you can have as much money as you want in the world, but without love, how happy can you be? Because if you try to buy it, it's not real.

EVE

Once we start loving each other and stop giving a f*ck about what this n*gga got on, or how he gettin' it, and when you start to love just being alive, you good. Live to build.

GHOSTFACE KILLAH OF WU-TANG CLAN

I want a man who's going to love me and treat me like number one.

LIL' KIM

Respecting how someone feels and understanding what they feel. Love is a compromising situation. To love somebody, you got to understand them. You got to respect their feelings and their heart.

MR. SERV-ON

Whatever is close to your heart, you want to cherish it—whether it be family, money, or whatever. Love is what you hold dear to your heart.

JA RULE

Real love is broke love. When you're broke, you'll find out who really loves ya.

LORD G

Something that you hold dear or close to you without being obsessed with it. A dude that's a killer may love to kill people, somebody that loves flowers may plant flowers. That word and the passion for what you do is still the same, but the action is different.

FREDDIE FOXXX

An honest feeling about really caring for somebody. Not being scared to tell somebody how you really feel.

RICHIE RICH

I'm on some other sh*t about sex. . . . I love the thought of having sex more than havin' it. I'd rather have a stimulating conversation with a woman now than f*ck. I'm not out to f*ck anybody. Now I place that low on my list of priorities.

DJ QUIK

I'm the kind of person who stays in a relationship for a long time. As women, we're gonna feel like we can't get over him. We're gonna feel unbalanced. But if you spend your lifetime being afraid and second-guessing yourself over a man, you'll never go anywhere.

KEISHA OF TOTAL

You just gotta look for what you are. If you look for that in a woman, you'll find her.

SNOOP DOGG

[B]ut I want to let women know that they don't need to let a bad situation keep them down and that they can go through a lot and still come out on top.

SOLÉ

Love. It can't be thirty-seventy. It's gotta be fifty-fifty. Both people gotta respect each other.

LIL' KIM

I don't need a guy to make me complete.

MISSY "MISDEMEANOR" ELLIOTT

A lot of people put sex as the first priority in they life. I mean, that's the worst thing that you can ever do. . . . But to me, right now, sex is not a priority. Bein' successful, bein' a good man, bein' a good fiancé, bein' a good father is what's important to me.

LUTHER "LUKE" CAMPBELL

It's harder to maintain a relationship than it is to get into one. It's real hard, but a n*gga gotta be knowing with their heart that this is what they want to do.

SNOOP DOGG

I've tried the "easy girl" approach, and that doesn't work. There's a line that has to be drawn, a certain level of respect that has to be met. The person who loves you the most should give you that space.

MARY J. BLIGE

I got most of my game from my mama. I've always told people that. She didn't necessarily teach me how to treat women, but she's a real woman, and being around her my whole life showed me what to expect in a real woman and how I should approach one.

SNOOP DOGG

It's the way he loves me. I love the way he loves me. I love waking up next to him.

DA BRAT

A guy's not getting it just like that. If there's no love and respect, what is there? Just sex? That wears thin.

MARY J. BLIGE

She may look nice, but does she have anything "up here"?

CANIBUS

I don't need a man to support me or keep me happy.

EVE

You've got to be able to deal with women on many different levels. If you are introduced to them physically before you are introduced to their ideas, sometimes you create problems for yourself.

STIC.MAN OF DEAD PREZ

If you love me, you're gonna love me for a long time, because I'm just being myself.

SILKK THE SHOCKER

When you love people, you don't wanna let them go, because you love them. It's hard to let them go—family members, boyfriends, girlfriends—but you just gotta, because if you keep them around, they'll drain you and try to hold you back.

MARY J. BLIGE

droppin' science

If that person isn't putting in the time and love and effort he should be, you need to back off for a minute. You need to be like "Let me step back for a little while. You do *you.* Come back when you're ready to do me."

FOXY BROWN

Makin' love is looking into your lover's eyes, feelin' their soul. Actually feeling their heart and feeling what they feel.

LIL' KIM

A person who's dealing with love is going to manifest that under any circumstances.

CAPPADONNA OF WU-TANG CLAN

Sexy is being a leader, not a follower.

SOLÉ

If you're in a relationship, put some effort into it. It's not compromising your masculinity to be romantic.

CARL THOMAS

Sexy is confidence, originality, not practiced. Sexy is natural.

LIL' ZANE

I realized I had to detach myself from certain people and certain things just to move on, to basically grow up and develop some type of self-love. When you running around and f*cking like ten girls a day, you ain't loving yourself.

TRAGEDY

It's important for you to love yourself before you can love anyone else.

DA BRAT

Sexy is not being beautiful. It's being confident.

DALVIN DEGRATE

The person I'm in love with is the person that I am with.

WYCLEF JEAN

Sexy is every woman with self-esteem.

MARY J. BLIGE

Love is loving yourself first and being careful of what you say to people and accepting what people do to you without letting it make you feel differently about yourself. That's where love starts at.

LIL' KIM

Love is high on my agenda . . . so love is something that is serious to me. Man/woman love is one of the most important things I've ever encountered. Men sometimes think cheating is our right and second nature to us. Guys are more fly-by-night; but if a woman cheats on a guy, that stuff just rips our heart out of the socket.

YOUNG ZEE OF THE OUTSIDAZ

droppin' science

I would rather have a woman that's a lot less attractive but [has] a good head on her shoulders and knows what I'm about, or is willing to get to know me, than a girl who just looks good."

SILKK THE SHOCKER

You just don't give it away.

JILL SCOTT

When you got a good woman at home, there's no need to go searching.

MISSY "MISDEMEANOR" ELLIOTT

Love is truly a spiritual experience where you give the essence of your being to someone.

KRS-ONE

Sexual energy burns up a lot of brainpower, and when you're constantly thinking about it, you waste more mental energy. When you focus on one woman, you get more energy and strength, more than a lot of n*ggas can imagine.

RZA OF WU-TANG CLAN

ON "FAM" AND TAKIN' CARE OF YOURS 8

Got love for my family, 'cause they mine . . .

METHOD MAN, "PERFECT WORLD,"
TICAL 2000: JUDGEMENT DAY

Once I had my son, I learned two things: it's very difficult to raise a child, and I don't want to have more children until I'm married for a long time.

XZIBIT

I love my mama. She wasn't strict, but she still used to give me a lot of ass whippings."

JUVENILE OF CASH MONEY MILLIONAIRES

If you've got kids, you've got to back up a little bit. At some point you have to ask yourself, "If I ain't here to raise them, who's gonna raise them?"

MACK 10

I could go on record and talk about all the expensive sh*t, 'cause I can get all that sh*t now. I could walk up in a jewelry store and I could just get laced, but I don't want to do that. That's not real to me. My babies can't eat that. My babies can't live off that. That's how I keep my sanity. I look at everything through my kids' eyes.

METHOD MAN OF WU-TANG CLAN

You need that base. When you're f*cked up, you need someone you feel like you can talk to.

JA RULE

[My stepfather] gave me a hard work ethic. He would never tell me what to do. He would just tell me my options.

JUVENILE OF CASH MONEY MILLIONAIRES

I wouldn't have to go out and sell drugs for myself if my pops was there and see that I'ma get locked up.

JA RULE

My father was the only person who was like "Do whatever you want to do that's gonna make you happy."

CHARLI BALTIMORE

Being a parent makes you appreciate your parents. It makes you think, "Damn, Mommy really went through some shit to take care of me," 'cause now you're taking care of another life.

BEANIE SIGEL

More than anything else, fatherhood has taken me out of the streets. I'm very careful about putting myself in situations that could potentially take me away from being a father to my children.

BUSTA RHYMES

[E]ncourage your kids to utilize their talents and gifts to the fullest, any gift they got—basketball, football, computers, art, whatever. Don't let their talent slip away.

BEANIE SIGEL

You can't change the world by your muthaf*ckin' self, but you can change the child you put into it.

XZIBIT

Grandmothers to me are the most special thing, just for the simple fact that they have been around for years. And no matter what it was, whether it was the Depression or racism or the back of the bus, they are still here.

DA BRAT

droppin' science

Establishing a closer relationship with my father has been one of the hardest decisions I've ever had to make. I chose to make history of our past and begin anew.

MONICA

You made it, took the time to make it, so take the time to take care of it.

XZIBIT

Life's struggles make you realize the importance of having a mother.

BLACK ROB

[Loyalty] means sticking with your people through thick and thin. The reward at the end of the day could be greater than what you're anticipating.

BUSTA RHYMES

I pray. I have a strong family support group, too. If I didn't have that, I don't think I could do this.

STRINGS

The most important thing to me right now is securing a future for my daughter. Because without her, nothing else matters.

RAH DIGGA

Y'all n*ggas is glorifying chains and b*tches, but my son is the most important thing to me.

XZIBIT

Family always comes first for me. Why? Because my family keeps me grounded and humble. My children don't care that I'm in the spotlight as a rap artist. They care more that Daddy is there for them when they need me to be.

DJ TONY TOUCH

Nothing is worth more to me than [my brother C-Murder's] life. So why should we argue about anything in life that's material?

SILKK THE SHOCKER

Ain't nuthin' stronger than the blood. All that other sh*t is mud.

CAPPADONNA OF WU-TANG CLAN

If I didn't have the love of my family, I know I'd be dead.

KOKANE

When you knuckle up, or make a fist, you need all the fingers to come together. If one finger ain't in, it ain't a fist.

GANXSTA RIDD OF BOO-YAA T.R.I.B.E.

Me and my pops is crazy close now. . . . Once I grew up and became a man, I started to understand why he did the things that he did.

XZIBIT

We as women need fathers. Men have to understand that their daughters are just as important as their sons.

QUEEN LATIFAH

droppin' science

My thing is to make sure that I tie my camel down first and foremost at my house as opposed to trying to save the world. I've got to make sure that my situation at the house is straight before I can go out and start teaching and preaching to other people.

ZAAKIR OF JURASSIC 5

We gotta teach the children every day, keep a song,
Show them the light, teach them right from wrong . . .

ERIC B. & RAKIM,
"TEACH THE CHILDREN,"
DON'T SWEAT THE TECHNIQUE

ON STAYIN' ON THE RIGHT PATH

9

Now I choose wisely.

LAURYN HILL

Don't be no follower, man, 'cause you'll go down fast. . . . Yo, man, you gotta do things for yourself. Think for yourself. Know right from wrong. 'Cause that's what I had to do. I had to learn right from wrong.

RAEKWON "THE CHEF" OF WU-TANG CLAN

Coming up, it wasn't the greatest for me. Being that I had no support . . . I had no family to back me up. I didn't have any big brothers, I ain't have no Pop."

BLACK ROB

I've been shot at, stabbed. All of that street sh*t . . . you don't have to go through that if you don't want to. The option is yours. You have to set high standards for yourself.

RAHZEL "THE GODFATHER OF NOYZE"

Don't ruin your whole life trying to fit in. I was really a good kid. It was the environment that made me twist for the worst.

FAT JOE

I got tired of going back to jail. I felt like I was missing out on a lot of my life. I spent much of my childhood in jail, so it's time for me to just straighten up and fly right.

BLACK ROB

We're showing people that we can be good people, but there's a lot of situations that can provoke you into not being good at all.

COLDHARD OF CRUCIAL CONFLICT

I don't hang in the same places as before, because I'm on probation. I don't need to get caught up in that sh*t.

B.G. OF CASH MONEY MILLIONAIRES

It's easy to do the wrong things.

DMX

Now I know that some things piss you off, but the best thing is to think about the positive.

DA BRAT

You gotta start doin' right for God now. . . . The whole science of life is being able to pick right from wrong.

GHOSTFACE KILLAH OF WU-TANG CLAN

[My stepfather] was the type who let me do the wrong thing so I could see that it wasn't right. Then he'd sit down and tell me the right way.

LIL' WAYNE

It's hard to walk a straight line when the track is laid down crooked.

CEE-LO OF GOODIE MOB

Somebody told me once, "Everything you get the wrong way, you going to lose," and sho' nuff I did. I decided it was time to change my ways.

MANNIE FRESH

droppin' science

It's all about just basically knowing yourself and being at peace with what you're dealing with.

RAEKWON "THE CHEF" OF WU-TANG CLAN

I'm not gonna get involved in anything that's not good for me.

TRAY DEEE OF THA EASTSIDAZ

I've come to the conclusion that if you're doing the right thing, God won't let bad things happen.

JOE "RUN" SIMMONS OF RUN-D.M.C.

I had to do a six-month sentence in jail for shooting off a gun. Once I got out, I was like "Think different, do something else." . . . As much as n*ggas say they hard, if that's being hard, I'm not hard. Being hard to me is staying on the outside. That's hard.

XZIBIT

Have a goal and a way out, because it's about having options. Once the law get their hands on you, you ain't got no more options.

NELLY

You have to be smart enough to know.

EMINEM

[I]f you do the right thing, you don't have nothin' to worry about. . . . And you can't get caught up into worrying about where you gonna be at today or tomorrow, 'cause ain't nothin' promised."

MASTER P, CEO OF NO LIMIT RECORDS

[N]o matter what you're going through, hold on to that sense of self. Hold on to that sense of direction and don't be swayed.

XCEL OF BLACKALICIOUS

Modesty and moderation, that's what's important.

TELA

I sit back, contemplate on everything before I make a decision. I move with caution.

LAYZIE BONE OF BONE THUGS-N-HARMONY

Like the man always says, "Any fool can learn from his own mistakes, but the wise man must learn from the mistakes of others."

RZA OF WU-TANG CLAN

I'm trying to show and introduce my fellow inmates, most of whom are young men, to [the] different attributes all humans need to succeed, including discipline, self-confidence, determination, faith, and a belief in God and yourself.

SHYNE

If you keep doing what you love, there's nothing people can do about it.

PETE ROCK

Our Father who art in Heaven,
I'm not ashamed to ask for
guidance at twenty-seven . . .

DMX, "READY TO MEET
HIM," *FLESH OF MY FLESH,
BLOOD OF MY BLOOD*

ON SPIRITUALITY

droppin' science

When I was a small child, I was very attached to God—I loved God. I'm at peace because I'm very clear now about what really matters. God is the center of everything that I do.

LAURYN HILL

When you get sick, you gonna call on God. When somebody['s] on their death bed, they gonna call on God. So why not just go to him now?

MASE

It's a lot harder to be spiritual and soulful than it is to be hard.

PHAROAHE MONCH

I'm a child of God, man. Right now I'm trying to be righteous, because when you're right, wrong can't prevail. For Snoop Dogg, it's just all about love right now.

SNOOP DOGG

It's no coincidence that we're still here. It's not the beats, the rhymes, the phat car, the house, women, or drugs. It's Jesus Christ. And that's what's missing in the hip hop industry: the Holy Spirit.

PARRISH SMITH OF EPMD

People don't know what they're missing. You can have all the money in the world, the hottest cars, the hottest houses, you could be the chief of this, the executive of this, but if you don't got your spirit right, there's always gonna be a little bit of emptiness inside. I make goals to win Grammys and all that. But I still believe the ultimate goal is to make it into heaven.

RODNEY "DARKCHILD" JERKINS

I go to sleep and it's like "Wait a minute, Missy. You can go to the party and you can do your photo shoots and your interviews, but you can't make yourself stay up five minutes to say your prayers?" *He's* the one that wakes me up. *He's* the one that takes me through the day.

MISSY "MISDEMEANOR" ELLIOTT

Faith is never blind. It simply sees the unseen and speaks of the unheard. It is faith that truly sees everything.

KRS-ONE

What matters to me is how I look in God's eyes. I would never want God to frown on me. If God frowns on you, you can hang it up.

KOOL G RAP

Only God knows what's better for Master P than Master P. With God, there ain't no limit.

MASTER P, CEO OF NO LIMIT RECORDS

If God gives you certain messages, you're supposed to deliver them. That's your duty. You can't just take your talent and bury it.

COMMON

I come from a real spiritual background, and my faith in God has a lot to do with me being able to go on each day. I realize that I can't keep living in the past.

MISSY "MISDEMEANOR" ELLIOTT

God plays a big role in my life. Without him, there's no me.

THA D OF 2ND II NONE

Believe in God, believe in goodness, and you can't go wrong.

HEAVY D

We pray every day.

[DAVID] STYLES OF THE LOX

When I do pray, I pray to the higher self. To the higher force of energy. You know sometimes in life you gotta go through hell to come out all right. So when I'm going through my hell, like, I look to Allah and my lessons . . .

GHOSTFACE KILLAH OF WU-TANG CLAN

I'm a 100 percent believer in God.

DAZ DILLINGER OF THA DOGG POUND

Keep in touch with God.

REDMAN OF WU-TANG CLAN

I don't even care what it is you're into, if you're into something with some sort of spiritual or moral code or some sort of value system, that's getting you to do right as far as God's law.

TALIB KWELI OF BLACK STAR

I always pray before I eat, sleep, or wake up. I want God to know that I will humble myself before him at any time.

BIZZY BONE OF BONE THUGS-N-HARMONY

I stay in tune with the Creator, and I realize that no matter what you go through, if you're doing the Creator's work, there's always some light at the end of the tunnel.

COMMON

I chose to live for Christ . . . people can really respect what you do, and at the same time [you can] big-up the Creator.

BB JAY

I ain't holy. I'm just trying to be righteous by being myself.

KAM

Keep God first. If I lead a peaceful life, the peace will come back to me.

SNOOP DOGG

It's easy to talk sh*t when you got a silver spoon in your mouth. Just like it's easy to find God when you got money.

PLANET ASIA OF CALI AGENTS
(March 30, 2000. *Rebirth* magazine: www.rebirthmag.com)

Just like there are different languages, there are different practices. As long as you are following the laws of nature and the laws of the universe and following righteous nature, meaning doing right, then you know who God is.

COMMON

droppin' science

Don't give up on God.

DJ QUIK

Pray.

DJ TONY TOUCH

I started praying a whole lot. I asked God to give me my happiness and spirit back, and it worked. For a minute I thought I could fix things, but God is the answer.

EVE

It's not about Cristal; it's about Christ-style!

BB JAY

The Lord sends you messages when He's ready and not necessarily when we are.

MASE

For a long time in my life, I didn't have my [sh*t] together . . . just doing stupid sh*t, not caring about anybody or even myself. But I have a great relationship with God now.

MACY GRAY

Whether you're Buddhist, Muslim, Yoruba, or whatever, as long as you believe in the Supreme Being and do right to people, that is what God is about.

COMMON

God walks with me throughout—that's the head of my life right now.

MYSTIKAL

You definitely need to have God in your life to give you that proper balance. It's needed to stay sane around this place.

TELA

I'm not the one to question anyone's path to God. If [Islam is] their religion and they're loving themselves—wholeheartedly following it and loving others as they love themselves—I can't knock no one's religion.

COMMON

I've always known that my powers didn't come from me, they came from somewhere else. It took some time for me to really establish my relationship with that force, which is God. I've been through situations where I had no choice but to give it up. And going through those things, you just can't forget, you can't be ungrateful."

SHYNE

Every time I get a check, I stay hollering at God, because I fear him. I'm grateful to the fullest.

E-40

We're not heavenly souls and spirits that can live perfectly. I'm not a spiritual leader; I just believe in God.

JA RULE

I believe God is everything in your heart and soul. He is what you believe him to be.

TRICK DADDY

You can lead a horse to water
　　but you can't make him drink,
You can lead a man to knowledge
　　but you can't make him think . . .

BLOOD OF ABRAHAM,
"TION," *EYEDOLLARTREE*

ON SCHOOLIN'
YA BIRD

[Teaching my son] just how to stand on his own two. Once you do that, you can conquer anything. When times is hard, things get rough, you be able to handle that sh*t.

REDMAN OF WU-TANG CLAN

[M]y writing came from my love for school. I was *really* into school. I cried when I got C's. I used to enjoy doing homework. I was a geek about school.

RAH DIGGA

If you don't know your past, you won't know your future.

THE LAST EMPEROR

Knowledge is important. Nobody can take nothin' away from you if you got knowledge.

RAEKWON "THE CHEF" OF WU-TANG CLAN

A "hot boy" is a n*gga about his paper. If you're in school, you're a hot boy.

BRYAN WILLIAMS OF BIG TYMERS

My parents were really strict when it came to education, so I *had* to go to school; I had to go to college, and I really appreciate that. It took a while before I got put on in the rap game, so I had to work as a professional illustrator before I got my chance to shine. I didn't have to resort to hustlin' drugs on the street. This was because I had a solid educational background. With both street knowledge and education from schooling, you can adapt to any situation.

MR. BOOKA-T OF SPOOKS

I'm a real advocate of education . . .

RAH DIGGA

Education is important no matter what field you want to go into. . . . Take your education seriously.

MARY J. BLIGE

When you learn more, you're more free to do things.

COMMON

If I didn't have some kind of education, I wouldn't be able to count my money!

MISSY "MISDEMEANOR" ELLIOTT

Master the art of English and math, so you can handle your business / and count your cash.

GRYM REAPER OF GRAVEDIGGAZ

Being a Big Willie is not about the car you drive. For me, the ultimate Willie measuring stick is intellect.

WILL SMITH

You've got to know who you are to know who you are not.

CEE-LO OF GOODIE MOB

Now I listen more and I watch more. I've realized that what other people is saying is important.

CANIBUS

droppin' science

I would love to be able to go back and say, "Look, yo, I got my education."

EMINEM

We gotta add on with some skills, 'cause when you talk about self-determination, that means you responsible for your own sh*t.

STIC.MAN OF DEAD PREZ

You need to know the foundations of anything.

EPMD

[My ex-wife and I] were kinda like high school sweethearts. But we both dropped out. It wasn't a f*cking wise decision for both of us to quit school, have a child together. . . .

EMINEM

I'm still trying to figure myself out, like most people . . . because I'm still living and learning . . .

LAURYN HILL

I would take book smarts over street smarts if I had to make a choice. Book smarts could get you to be the CEO of a company, own an oil company, be like Donald Trump, and I don't know if street smarts could get you anywhere but the penitentiary.

ICE-T

Knowledge really is power.

I wish I would have stayed in school. I did a bid instead. I think no matter how you get an education, it's important that you get it. I went to jail, dropped out of school, but while in jail I got both my GED and thirty college credits.

CAPONE OF CAPONE-N-NOREAGA

Better get a good education, man.

MC REN

Stay in school.

RAEKWON "THE CHEF" OF WU-TANG CLAN

Street smarts will get you killed sooner than book smarts. Street smarts will teach you how to make money, but 98 percent of how you do it is illegal. You can't retire on street smarts, but you can on book smarts.

ICE-T

Everybody should finish high school as well as college. Why? Because you need knowledge of all types in order to get through this life. It's important that you do get an education; it's important that you know as much as you can.

BIANCA OF MAJOR FIGGAS

We decided we wanted to do something different. We started reading so we wouldn't be like the average rap group out here with no guidance.

ALI OF ST. LUNATICS

droppin' science

I believe that education is very important, but there are different types of education. Of course, there's public schools, secondary schools, and college; but then there's also street knowledge, which I feel is very important as well, because of the way I grew up. I grew up poor and in the ghetto. Street knowledge helped me to survive.

MR. BOOKA-T OF SPOOKS

Stay in school, do not use drugs, and stay focused, because no one can take a good education away from you."

LIL' BOW WOW

Although school seems corny when you're young, knowledge over ignorance will win always.

ICE-T

You always want to learn something. It's just in our nature. It's unnatural to not want to learn.

TALIB KWELI OF BLACK STAR

If we are to affect the minds of people, we have to do it through institutions such as schools.

KRS-ONE

ON OVERCOMIN'
AND ACHIEVIN' 12

I come correct and I won't look back
'Cause it ain't where you're from, it's where you're at . . .

ERIC B. & RAKIM, "IN THE GHETTO,"
LET THE RHYTHM HIT 'EM

droppin' science

You can do anything you want.

GZA "THE GENIUS" OF WU-TANG CLAN

It ain't easy, but I've got goals. And I'm going to step forth and do all of them.

MISSY "MISDEMEANOR" ELLIOTT

I was a ghetto prisoner, all my n*ggas were ghetto prisoners, and we still are ghetto prisoners to some degree. But we have to rise mentally so we don't get caught up and be stagnant with the same old thoughts. . . . We really can have a big impact on the whole world if we just use our brains and make sh*t happen.

NAS

I want to be ownin' things. I want to go to a whole 'nother level that no other female is doing it at.

FOXY BROWN

The 'hood's got talent, any 'hood. That's the bottom right there, you can only excel from there.

PRODIGY OF MOBB DEEP

You have to keep getting bigger and bigger goals. You'll fall when you're satisfied and cool with where you're at. Just keep it going, keep it moving.

FAT JOE

I spent so many days in my room—years and years of sorting out my problems conditioned me. So that when things happen, I don't care how good or bad it is, I can adapt to it.

LISA "LEFT EYE" LOPES OF TLC

That's why our people got to get to a point where we realize the economic importance of owning our own. Too many people are talking about success, but we got to strive for success.

WILLIE D OF THE GETO BOYS

I'm an observer. I look at what I set to achieve, and then do my thing.

INSPECTAH DECK OF WU-TANG CLAN

I speak loud and I'm really fearless.

CHUCK D

I wanna give back a message . . . the message is a lot more valuable than giving a community center. That'll go under. They'll forget all about it. They don't know what a community center is. Give them a message, and they will have that with them when they walk the streets.

DMX

No one has a choice where they grew up or what color they are. If you're a rich kid or a ghetto kid, you have no control over your circumstance. The only control you have is to get out of your situation or stay in it.

EMINEM

This [the rap game] is all I got. I ain't graduate from high school. I dropped out in the tenth grade. My life is surrounded by rap. Besides that, I got the streets. And I be damned if I go back there.

B.G. OF CASH MONEY MILLIONAIRES

droppin' science

I seen way beyond my boundaries when I was coming up. I always had vision.

KOOL G RAP

Yo, I failed ninth grade three times, but I don't think it was necessarily 'cause I'm stupid. I didn't go to school. I couldn't deal.

EMINEM

When all looked like it was lost, things kind of came up. It's amazing.

PRINCE PAUL

I'm the type of person I'm liable to do anything. If I'm in a hopeless and desperate situation, I'm gonna do anything I can to get outta that situation. I just won't accept it.

JAY-Z

There's always gonna be n*ggas in the projects. There's always gonna be n*ggas strugglin'. There's always gonna be motherf*ckers striving to get ahead and be a better motherf*cker.

MC EIHT

My million ain't the last million out there. Go and get yours!

DJ QUIK

In my neighborhood, there wasn't nothing to do but sell drugs, do drugs, or watch TV.

LIL' WAYNE OF CASH MONEY MILLIONAIRES

I can be much more than I am. I wasn't using my strengths properly. I was using my strengths to try to be a better drug dealer when I could've been using them to try to be a better MC.

JA RULE

I try to focus on my quality, and I don't compromise what I believe in to get it.

MOS DEF OF BLACK STAR

It's all about being consistent, staying focused no matter what you are, black, white, Spanish, whatever. Come thorough, come official. Don't ever be intimidated or feel like once you get turned away it's over. You just gotta keep it moving.

DJ TONY TOUCH

I've calmed down a lot. I used to be mad hostile, but you can't be like that, especially in business . . .

JU-JU OF THE BEATNUTS

Don't sit around and just be crying or be mad about your situation. Go out there and do your thing.

NAS

I stayed focused on my school and my raps. I didn't let the projects take me under.

JUVENILE OF CASH MONEY MILLIONAIRES

You only live once, man. Do what you really wanna do.

PLANET ASIA

My grandma told me there's always work to be done.

AMIR "?UESTLOVE" THOMPSON OF THE ROOTS

I'd rather do something different and fail than do something mediocre and succeed.

LITTLE X (HIP HOP VIDEO DIRECTOR)

I was strugglin', man, it ain't no secret. I ain't have the silver spoon in my mouth. Everybody have their problems in life. You just gotta know how to deal with it.

JUVENILE OF CASH MONEY MILLIONAIRES

You gotta believe in yourself and don't give up, number one! [It's important] to have a good heart, good intentions, and good people around you who will support you. Stay ambitious, don't be lazy . . . don't sleep all day!

RAEKWON "THE CHEF" OF WU-TANG CLAN

When you really believe in what you're doing, it always prevails.

LIL' TROY

You know, I'm not the smartest person that you ever met. I'm not Einstein or nothing like that. But I'm a person that always thinks that he gonna do something, and I think that's the difference.

MASTER P, CEO OF NO LIMIT RECORDS

You have to search yourself and give it your all, and if it don't work, you can't give up. You have to get your face off the floor, put one foot in front of the other, and keep on going.

DA BRAT

I feel like everybody goes through certain things in their life because it's how you learn, it's how you get to where you need to be. Sometimes you say to yourself, "Did I really have to go through all that to get here?" But that's what makes you realize, "I can do anything."

SOLÉ

It was a struggle for our parents, so we didn't have high aspirations, but we knew that there was hope to overcome our situation.

TRAY DEEE OF THA EASTSIDAZ

I'm striving for perfection.

RAEKWON "THE CHEF" OF WU-TANG CLAN

You can either dwell on the problem or figure out the solution.

THA D OF 2ND II NONE

What I learned from the whole experience [of attending an exclusive girls' school] was that there's more to life than what's around the way. I saw a whole 'nother level of income brackets that put into my head, "Okay, I want more in life. There's a whole 'nother life of luxury that exists beyond the local way." I was determined to go out and get it.

RAH DIGGA

It's sad that enough of us don't take the initiative to control our own destiny. It's like we're waiting on *they*. That's the oldest excuse in the book, *waiting on they*.

CEE-LO OF GOODIE MOB

droppin' science

The best way to deal with the bad examples is to show 'em a good example.

BUN B (AKA U.G.K.)

You can do anything.

STRINGS

Everybody has to find a role model or someone to look up to.

KRAYZIE BONE OF BONE THUGS-N-HARMONY

I just feel like you have to get yourself together and have some serious plans for the future. You can't just live for the moment.

T-BOZ OF TLC

I think the more problems I have, the more positive I become, because it gives me the confidence that I can handle the next problem. My strength comes from witnessing that things can always get better.

MYA

If people take anything from my music, it should be motivation to know that anything is possible as long as you keep working at it and don't back down. I didn't have nothin' going for me . . . school, home . . . until I found something I loved . . . and that changed everything.

EMINEM

If you wanna stay paid, you gotta do work, you gotta hustle.

BUN B (AKA U.G.K.)

Everybody else play by "their" rules. And you know people wanna keep you out, but they can't keep you out when you're tight, when your game's tight, when you got a good strategy.

MASTER P, CEO OF NO LIMIT RECORDS

I've learned you just got to keep going and do your thing.

MACY GRAY

You gotta get hungry, create new goals, new ambitions, new motivations.

FAT JOE

Dust yourself off and try again.

DA BRAT

I get the butterflies and go through stages and overcome it and deal with it. I face my fears. . . . 'Cause when I face my fears, it takes a load off my brain. By facing your fears, you actually will have no fear. By facing 'em, you cancel them out.

CANIBUS

We try to pay attention to the mistakes that we make ourselves and that other people make. But we try to keep, most of all, in our own minds, what we're here for, and that's to better ourselves. We're always about self-determination. In anything you do, it's a process to elevate.

COCOA BROVAZ

I hold on to times when I had to struggle. That's the science of going through hell and having to come out right—because everybody gots to go through hell to come out right.

GHOSTFACE KILLAH OF WU-TANG CLAN

I'm a survivor, I'm a warrior! This is my life, I have no choice but to make it in this!

FAT JOE

Always stick to your dreams and keep your head up.

KURUPT OF THA DOGG POUND

You get a lot further if you look at yourself when things go wrong.

POSDNOUS OF DE LA SOUL

The first purpose in life is to get yourself in order. Before you can solve any problem, you must first solve the problem within yourself. You must first find you before you can find anything else.

KILLAH PRIEST OF WU-TANG CLAN

Everything goes in circles. You just have to wait for your time.

LORD JAMAR OF BRAND NUBIAN

I've done some things I wish I could have handled better. But . . . people make mistakes, man. You learn from them.

EMINEM

So live how you know how to live and direct your energies toward creating the person that you want to be, not trying to emulate others.

JERU THE DAMAJA

I haven't achieved everything I want, and I definitely want a lot more. . . . There's a desire to improve what I've built thus far and make it better.

LL COOL J

You have to be prepared to lose all before you gain anything.

RAH DIGGA

I became a little older, and then I realized that you could be whatever you wanted to be.

SILKK THE SHOCKER

Anything you want, you can get. Don't think there's nothing you want that you can't get. If you live a regular life, doing the things you know are right, and they're things you know you should do, then you're gonna have a good life.

YOUNG ZEE OF THE OUTSIDAZ

The only progress that we can make is that if each person tries to better themselves.

KIMANI OF THE MASTERMINDS
(April 16, 2000. *Rebirth* magazine: www.rebirthmag.com)

Every army that goes to war uses a strategy. Every company that seeks something or is trying to get ahead, there's a strategy to everything. And it's all about working that plan, putting that strategy together.

THIRSTIN HOWL III

Big Tymers is a state of mind. If you gonna do something, do it big-time. If you gonna get a car, go big-time with it. If you gonna go to school and graduate, go big-time with it. A Big Tymer is the one that's on. They are the leader, not the follower.

MANNIE FRESH OF BIG TYMERS

Try not to sleep on your destiny.

NAS

Never give up. Never lose sight of what you want to do. And never let any obstacle hold you back.

KANE & ABEL

Just because you come from the projects don't mean that you can't be on the honor roll.

GHOSTFACE KILLAH OF WU-TANG CLAN

[Y]ou have to learn how to fall. Get back up and put one foot in front of the other and keep on going and try to keep learning from your mistakes.

DA BRAT

You can do anything you want to in this world if you apply your mind, your determination, and a little sweat. You can make it happen.

ICE CUBE

You gotta go through hell to come out right.

GHOSTFACE KILLAH OF WU-TANG CLAN

So if you really have something that you want to do, you can be that . . . but you just got to have insight enough to see what that is and go achieve it. It's going to take work, but anything is truly possible.

Q-TIP

In every situation that's worthwhile, you have to pay dues. You don't always recognize that when it's happening.

DILATED PEOPLES

The main thing is to never let anything tear you down mentally. Struggling gives life its balance. Without the struggle, success wouldn't be that enjoyable.

THIRSTIN HOWL III

I definitely straightened my sh*t up after I got shot. . . . So I turned it all around and started going to school, got my little diploma and whatnot.

SHYNE

[N]o matter what you're going through, hold on to that sense of self. Hold on to that sense of direction and don't be swayed.

XCEL OF BLACKALICIOUS

I love a challenge! So even when something gets me mad or knocks me down, I can still come back and fight and smile.

LIL' ZANE

[B]ut if you wanna make it somewhere in life, you're going to have to overcome a lot of hardships. Nothing comes easy.

LUDACRIS

Even when you get the worst news possible, you still stay optimistic and say, "Yo, I can beat this." Instead of "Damn, I'm going to die." 'Cause when you tell yourself that you're going to die, that's what usually happens. That's the power of our own minds, the power of our own words.

POETIC OF GRAVEDIGGAZ

The times were so hard [growing up], it's something you never wanna go back to. No toilet paper. No doorknobs on the doors. Holes in the ceiling. Roaches everywhere. That's what I grew up in. That's what motivates me to get my paper every day . . .

TOMMY WRIGHT III

It's not where you're from, it's where your head's at.

SEAN PAUL OF THE YOUNGBLOODZ

I've learned from everything that I've done and I don't regret anything.

EVE

Everything happens for a reason. . . . What don't kill you can only make you stronger.

JAY-Z

I don't believe in failure. I believe that if you truly give it your all, and you're not bullsh*tting yourself, you'll eventually succeed. The only two things I wanted to do in life were to become an illustrator and to make records, and I had the opportunity to do both because I gave it my all. You just have to be focused.

MR. BOOKA-T OF SPOOKS

If you keep doing what you love, there's nothing people can do about it.

PETE ROCK

Don't try to get what the next man has. Be your own superstar. Do you!

LIL' MO

[E]verything comes with a struggle, so I'm glad I struggled. I've struggled all my life, but God always made a way for me.

QUEEN PEN

I was too determined [to succeed] in life to be a failure.

TRINA

ON FAME AND SUCCESS 13

Keep risin' to the top, yeahhh . . .

SEAN "P. DIDDY" COMBS,
"DON'T STOP WHAT
YOU'RE DOING," *NO WAY OUT*

Always remember: if you have a dream, don't think somebody else is obligated to help you out on you being successful, 'cause you make that happen. If you see somebody waiting on something, it's because they're undecided on what they're about to do.

NELLY

Every kid wants something positive to happen in life. . . . We all come from being dirt poor to being success stories. You can do what we did. It's not impossible.

FAT JOE

I believe I can do anything if I put my mind to it. No matter how difficult things may seem or become, I just always work and set a goal.

LL COOL J

No matter what in life, people, money, and situations change, especially when you're trying to achieve a goal. True success in life is measured in self-respect and the respect you receive from others for the way you go about doing things.

SAUKRATES

Life is much more hectic now because there are less cracks in the wall. There are less hiding places, places where I can just be me and see what I used to see. It hurts, in a way, because I can't be as close to my people anymore as I'd like to be.

DMX

Don't get a big head; stay f*cking humble. 'Cause the biggest motherf*ckers I know—from Dre to Rza to Snoop—are regular people. And they're the coolest, nicest gentlemen that I know.

DJ MUGGS OF SOUL ASSASSINS/CYPRESS HILL

I always wanted to complete something I started. I feel like everybody has a plan, but only the smart people are prepared to execute their plan and make it work for them.

DR. DRE

I'm getting everything because I worked hard for mine.

JA RULE

I always thought "game" was just a replacement word for knowledge when you're in the streets. I analyzed it in and out, through and front. To say you have game means that you *know;* been there, experienced it. People can point things out to you, show you little different angles to make money and all that kind of stuff. But nobody can really give you the game. You gotta go out there and acquire it yourself.

TOO $HORT

There's always room to grow. I've reached certain goals, but there's always room to grow.

MACK 10

Ego is what destroys every man in the world. Pride and ego.

MASE

Success is not a destination when you stop; success is a journey till you die.

MR. NITRO

91

droppin' science

You got to take a chance.

LIL' CEASE

When you start getting successful and sh*t, and you start believing things about yourself . . . it's up to you to click that switch off.

JA RULE

When you have nothing, you want to be glorified.

BENZINO OF MADE MEN

I used to have this motto: you think big, be big.

CHA CHA

You only get to live once, so set the goals and make it happen.

DA BRAT

Right now, we're putting in the work so we can bear the fruits of that work. We're not going to stop until we get there.

JUVENILE OF CASH MONEY MILLIONAIRES

It's all about timing. If [success] is supposed to happen, it will. And if it's not, it won't. Everything that happens in life is God's plan.

CASE

[Having success is] hard because you have a lot of jealousy and envy, and there's a lot of people who won't let you get big if they can't get big.

WARREN G

What I do know is that you have to believe in yourself first, before you can get anyone else to believe in you.

DA BRAT

Sometimes I think I am [overscrutinized], but that comes with the territory, so I don't really complain about it. I just gotta handle it. I'm blessed to be where I am. That's one of the things that comes with success."

SEAN "P. DIDDY" COMBS

It's not about riches, it's about what you are gonna do with your life. . . . With a good plan, you can accomplish anything.

VINNIE BROWN OF NAUGHTY BY NATURE

The real will come to life. When you really believe in what you're doing, it always prevails.

LIL' TROY

But the whole thing is walking with your head up, never walking with your head down. Going out there, doing a lot of footwork, and not thinking that you're gon' blossom overnight. You gon' have some ups and downs, but you gotta crawl before you walk.

E-40

You have to keep striving and working hard, keep on going after what you want.

WARREN G

I'm a mental dude, I like the challenge. Everything I do, I try to master it. Even the small things.

JAY-Z

You gotta be able to stay away from negativity and surround yourself with real muthaf*ckas and positive muthaf*ckas and muthaf*ckas that got goals.

E-40

I don't take fame too seriously. I used to. When I was young. But it was painful.

Q-TIP

Look, I work hard, but you've got to play just as hard.

QUEEN LATIFAH

Fame is a blessing and a curse at the same time, but either way you look at it, you gotta humble yo'self.

DRE OF OUTKAST

Keep your focus and don't let nobody change your mind. . . . Just keep on goin'.

YOUNG BLEED

When you give, you get. You'll be blessed if you give. I just want it all, so I can help everybody else.

DA BRAT

I just ended up, you know, finding out that there is *always* another route. If you can't get it this way, Duke, there is another way to get it.

BUSTA RHYMES

I set my goals high. I make the best of what I'm doing . . . you gotta keep working.

JUVENILE OF CASH MONEY MILLIONAIRES

Everyone doubts you're gonna make it until you do something good.

BONE SKANLESS OF SKANBINO MOB

Don't never let anyone take you out [of] your game. . . . If you feel as though you really know you can do it, then stick with it.

DRAG-ON

You don't always have to be way on the top to be somebody or to accomplish what you're trying to do.

PRINCE PAUL

I'm happy that I did what I did. So other Latino kids could at least see that I did it and not feel like they can't do it. I'm not so much a role model but more like someone you could relate to. I defied the odds.

BIG PUN

Just stay true and everything will work itself out.

SNOOP DOGG

Accepting the fruits of success also means to accept the loss of success.

SOLÉ

I got a f*ckin' problem with losin'. I have high expectations in everything I do. If I go right now to play Tiger Woods in golf, I expect to beat his ass.

LUTHER "LUKE" CAMPBELL

[T]o me, the best revenge in the world is success.

SUGE KNIGHT, CEO OF DEATH ROW RECORDS

All I really care about is being a happy mother, a healthy woman, a good wife, and an all-around good person.

T-BOZ OF TLC

I try to walk around with a feeling of gratitude and humility in my heart that's accompanied by some faith and determination and some confidence, but no arrogance. I think that has a lot to do with it, because the seeds you plant, that's the harvest you're going to reap.

LL COOL J

You have to build your foundation solid. You can't start from the top, you have to start from the bottom if you want to build. . . . You need a team. That's the only way you can come up in this world is learning how to work together.

SOUTH PARK MEXICAN

Consistency is the key to success.

50 CENT

You gotta go through some hell sometimes for sh*t to come out right. That's why I am where I am today.

BUSTA RHYMES

If you're gonna make it, you gotta get up off your butt and make it happen. That's what I did.

RARA

Whatever you wanna do in life, keep your head straight and stay focused on what you want to do. And if your number-one dream don't work, go for your number two. One of 'em gonna happen.

WARREN G

We can stay focused on what we want. We try to look at the next decade rather than the next year. What we started doing is asking ourselves better questions and getting better answers.

DJ MUGGS OF SOUL ASSASSINS/CYPRESS HILL

The only thing that separates us from success is fear. And the only thing that overcomes fear is faith.

LL COOL J

Do what you gotta do, yo. F*ck [whoever] laughs at you, f*ck [whoever] feels like you ain't down because you ain't got the newest Jordans and all that sh*t.

FREDDIE FOXXX

I attribute [my career success] to having no Plan B. No other plan of survival. A sense of determination that's so extreme, I can't accept failure as an option.

BUSTA RHYMES

Everything changes and nothing changes. So much of my life hasn't changed at all. All my issues are still there . . .

MACY GRAY

I don't believe in luck. I believe everything happens for a reason. You make happen what you want to happen.

NELLY

Don't nothing come to a sleeper but a dream.

MACK 10

I pride myself on not getting caught up in the game, like I'm no superstar. Because stars fall, and you know it's true that you are doing big things, but remember your folks, and I pride myself on that.

JT MONEY

Success is everything you ever wanted in life, everything you've ever worked hard for.

NAS

[F]ame isn't real. Making an impression upon the hearts and minds and the spirit of humanity, that's real.

LL COOL J

Being successful is a state of mind. Success begins with the person from within. A successful person can be a street sweeper. It all comes on different levels. True success begins with happiness. You're successful when you're happy. It all depends on what you're looking for and what you need. When you're successful, there's not too much more that you want. If you're spiritual, have a great family, have a fulfilling career, then you're successful.

YOUNG ZEE OF THE OUTSIDAZ

Life is like checkers. You've got to make the right moves, like double-jumpin' the next man when he's making his moves. You can't be too relaxed.

DRAG-ON

You have to have faith in God, you have to stay committed, and you have to have emotional, mental, and physical stamina. That's important. I do what I do based on that.

LL COOL J

[S]tudy the game, analyze it, be honest and dedicated, be persistent and creative, but most importantly, follow your dream.

GURU OF GANG STARR

If I let fame get the best of me, I'm going to self-destruct. And I don't want to self-destruct.

EMINEM

Whatever you wanna do, keep God in your life. Pray all the time. Pay your dues and just work hard. Give it 110 percent every time you do something.

WARREN G

droppin' science

I got into this to make music. I didn't get into it for interviews or pictures or videos. To me, that just distracts me from my music. I don't give a f*ck about the fame.

DJ MUGGS OF SOUL ASSASSINS/CYPRESS HILL

[Y]ou've got to stay focused. . . . It's focus, in my opinion, and that's what I want to say to anybody who has any desire to build anything that's real.

RUSSELL SIMMONS, CEO OF DEF JAM RECORDS

I never waited for anybody to give me anything. If I wanted something, I knew that I was gonna have to be the one to go out and get it, because wasn't nothing just coming to the nigga like me. Opportunities didn't come my way. I had to chase them.

JAY-Z

I always had high expectations.

MACK 10

Being famous ain't about finally doing things the way you always wanted to. It's the toughest game you can play. You've got to stay sharp, you know what I'm sayin'? You find out real quick what they mean when they say it's lonely at the top.

SNOOP DOGG

It takes sacrifice. It's not impossible to achieve, but you gotta prepare for it if you do. That's one thing, can't nobody prepare you for it.

NELLY

If you put in 100 percent, you are going to get 100 percent back.

PSYCHO LES
OF THE BEATNUTS

If you've been dedicated for so long, I believe success is bound to happen. Not only in music, but all aspects of life.

HI-TEK

14

ON MAKIN' "BANK"

With the window cracked, holler back, money ain't a thang . . .

JAY-Z, "MONEY AIN'T A THANG," *HARD KNOCK LIFE*

Money definitely helps your situation. I'm not going to tell a kid not to get money and better his or her life. But at the same time, money is not going to end your problems. If anything, it's going to create new problems.

SEAN "P. DIDDY" COMBS

Money ain't no joke. You've gotta respect money and spend time with your money, man. You gotta respect it, 'cause if you don't, it will be gone.

DJ MUGGS OF SOUL ASSASSINS/CYPRESS HILL

Money isn't everything, especially when you're without someone you love.

LIL' KIM

I manage my money right. I save as much money as I can.

JUVENILE OF CASH MONEY MILLIONAIRES

At the end of the day, money can't buy you love or happiness. . . . At the end of the day, all that matters is whether or not you win.

SEAN "P. DIDDY" COMBS

I want to make my money work for me and not always work for the money.

EVE

That's the whole thing about success—you could have all the money in the world, but if you don't have peace of mind, and if you're not enjoying your life, then what you got it for?

JUVENILE OF CASH MONEY MILLIONAIRES

When you get money, you gotta be smart.

HAVOC OF MOBB DEEP

I just try to explain to my oldest daughter that this is for her. I really look at it from that perspective. I'm making sure that her future is straight. She knows Mommy got to pay her tuition.

CHARLI BALTIMORE

I works for mine.

JUVENILE OF CASH MONEY MILLIONAIRES

Money is a necessity that yo eed to survive and get what you need out here. Power? If you have the power, you are going to get the money anyway.

MASTER P, CEO OF NO LIMIT RECORDS

For me, it ain't the funds ya got, it's how long ya got it.

ICE-T

Every young person wants it all, and you don't have to sell drugs to get it. You have to pay your dues, stay on the right track, and master what you want to do. I don't have everything. Not that I ever expect to get it. But I am in control of my own destiny, and that's the most important thing.

WARREN G

droppin' science

It's cool to have money, but you got to have morals, too. I can go to sleep every night 'cause I know I didn't f*ck with anybody to get it. That sh*t is important to me. Before I had cash, I was a million-dollar n*gga in my heart already.

MACK 10

People get this illusion that if you're successful and make a lot of money, your problems go away. If anything, they double. . . . Oh sure, we've got the money to move or live anywhere, have nice cars, and sh*t like that . . . but certain things don't go away.

B REAL OF CYPRESS HILL

Everybody ain't jiggy. Some of us strive for more than just the material aspects of life.

ZIN

You know, if you're a white person, you've seen the Kennedys, the Rockefellers, the Rothschilds. You have history pictures of white people living affluently. You go to golf courses. You've been invited to country clubs. We haven't—you know what I'm saying?

SEAN "P. DIDDY" COMBS

So all the Rollies and the nice clothes, that sh*t is dope, but come on, don't take it to that extreme.

FATAL HUSSEIN OF THE OUTLAWS

Money isn't everything. . . . I'd rather have respect than be the richest man in the world.

JADAKISS OF THE LOX

Money doesn't change your color. It doesn't change anything but your worth, which is based off a popular, established view of how much a piece of paper is worth.

PHARELL WILLIAMS OF THE NEPTUNES

Save your money.

DARRYL "D.M.C." MCDANIELS OF RUN-D.M.C.

I'm trying to get mine because my family is full of poverty. I got a lot of motherf*ckers I gotta look out for.

JUVENILE OF CASH MONEY MILLIONAIRES

What I'm saying is "Go ahead and get your money, get your juice, but don't get caught up."

KRS-ONE

Life, not money, is the real wealth.

KK OF 2ND II NONE

Money frees you up to do things. . . . And it lets you do things for people, it can better the people's lives around you, and that's a good feeling.

JAY-Z

Get yours like I got mine. That's what my daddy taught me.

JUVENILE OF CASH MONEY MILLIONAIRES

droppin' science

Just because you make it don't mean you have to throw it away. Being tight is how rich people stay rich.

B.G. OF CASH MONEY MILLIONAIRES

[P]eople are under the wrong assumption about what wealth is. Because wealth is not anything on this earth, wealth is of the mind.

PHARELL WILLIAMS OF THE NEPTUNES

I take my last breath every time I hit the meth . . .

SEAN "P. DIDDY" COMBS

ON *NOT* GETTIN' BLUNTED

15

Can't get nothing done being drunk all the time.

DEL THA FUNKEE HOMOSAPIEN

I sniffed half of Peru, and I smoked the other half. That's what everybody did. So I did drugs. I barely remember the eighties.

RUSSELL SIMMONS, CEO OF DEF JAM RECORDS

I've finally realized I can't smoke five blunts a day and still handle sh*t. You can't act like you're still on the block when it comes to doing business.

NAS

We're not susceptible to those types of things [drugs] anymore. We evolved in the game. We beat it. And if you out there on some type of drug, you need to get yourself clean and get yourself right.

LAYZIE BONE OF BONE THUGS-N-HARMONY

I battled alcoholism. It just got to the next level, and I really didn't want to present myself to the world like that. I've got five children.

BIZZY BONE OF BONE THUGS-N-HARMONY

It's all a part of being young. A lot of them is on drugs. Yes you are. I am talking about you. You all taking Ecstasy, smoking cocaine. Smoking weed, drinking, having unprotected sex. You're f*cking idiots, man. Basically, you're f*cking idiots. You are throwing your f*cking life away. Then, when you get older, you have got nothing but regrets. . . . You can get wild and sh*t, but have some discretion. You don't know sh*t. Don't play yourself to where it's detrimental to your health.

METHOD MAN OF WU-TANG CLAN

Don't take drugs.

SAAFIR

Motherfuckas be in a zone with all the drinking and smoking, but it's deeper than that. That sh*t is destroying who we are. . . . We gotta cut all the bullsh*t out.

PRODIGY OF MOBB DEEP

I don't smoke weed no more. I just felt like [when I was] smoking weed, I wasn't as focused on my work and in my business aspect.

MISSY "MISDEMEANOR" ELLIOTT

It's the weak and the cowardly that depend on drugs every day.

SOUTH PARK MEXICAN

A sober mind is the best mind to have.

TURK OF CASH MONEY MILLIONAIRES

Don't go against the grain if
you can't handle it . . .

WU-TANG CLAN,
"THE GRAVEL PIT,"
THE W

ON TAKIN' A STAND AND
BEIN' INDEPENDENT

16

droppin' science

Be a leader. You don't have to fit in to be the bomb. You can be you, and you will gather followers.

RAH DIGGA

You gotta be able to stand on your own two, be a man and do it on your own.

PRODIGY OF MOBB DEEP

The biggest challenge is to be new and creative, 'cause that's the only way that you can further the genre. It will never get anywhere if everybody just clones everybody else.

CASE

You can't worry about what somebody think about you or what society say 'bout you. That's a speed breaker in yo' life. You gotta liberate yourself. No matter what you goin' through, you gotta keep goin'.

KHUJO OF GOODIE MOB

I used to get in trouble every day. I was trying to survive. You know, dealing with peer pressure. When you get caught up in peer pressure, it can lead you into a lot of trouble.

MASTER P, CEO OF NO LIMIT RECORDS

I'm a loner. I like being by myself sometimes.

PRINCE PAUL

I don't want to be reliant on anyone but myself.

MYA

If you can't stand up in the battlefield, then you ain't gonna make it.

TURK OF CASH MONEY MILLIONAIRES

Be sure not to let anyone control you.

KAY GEE OF NAUGHTY BY NATURE

If you call yourself a man, stand up for what you believe; stand up for your views; don't just sit there and let things happen—especially if you have a voice that people will listen to.

J-LIVE

[T]here are principles to everything that I do.

FREDDIE FOXXX

I just think you have to have the heart to follow your heart.

DJ QUIK

The man who goes left when everybody else is going right usually wins.

ERICK SERMON

I think it's more interesting to do something that has not been done before than to follow everyone else.

STYLES OF THE MOUNTAIN BROTHERS

droppin' science

You gotta take care of your business. . . . Don't think that nobody's gonna take care of your business for you. You gotta do it yourself.

GANGSTA OF THE COMRADS

Be independent.

CHUCK D

You can't live your life by what people say, anyway. . . . You got to do what's logical for you and what's good for you.

[DAVID] STYLES OF THE LOX

Find your own path.

LL COOL J

Be who you want to be.

LUTHER "LUKE" CAMPBELL

You just got to live your life.

BIG BOI

I was never cool. I've always been on some other sh*t. I refuse to conform to the status quo.

SHYNE

When I was in the street, I used to be like "How do these b*tches be having these cars and get up and go to work every day?" . . . Now I have respect for women that work and take care of their bills and responsibilities, because it's hard, but it also keeps you away from the bullsh*t.

AMIL

I grew up in a household that taught me the value of [a] good work ethic and being self-sufficient, because at the end of the day, you can't rely on too many things outside of your own.

BUSTA RHYMES

Communication, to me, is the biggest area for getting people on their own two feet.

CHUCK D

This is all about bein' original. If you ain't original, you ain't sh*t.

KRAYZIE BONE OF BONE THUGS-N-HARMONY

You know, freedom is all in the mind. If your mind is free, then you will always be free.

SHYNE

Let everybody know where you stand, because what makes the world go 'round is the differences in people. Everybody can't be the same or else nobody would breathe.

TALIB KWELI OF BLACK STAR

['C]ause bein' street struck'll get you
Nuttin' but a bullet or jail time.

BIG L, "STREET STRUCK,"
LIFESTYLES OV DA
POOR AND DANGEROUS

ON DOIN'
A "BID" 117

It ain't cool to go up. If you glorify prison, you better guess again and think twice, because all that sh*t you see on TV is fiction.

TRAGEDY KHADAFI

We're trying to tell these kids out there that if you do that petty sh*t, then you gone have to suffer the consequences, and that there ain't no fun in going to the pen.

E-ROCK OF 5TH WARD BOYZ

That jailhouse just made me sit down and think day for day that I really have something to live for. I just had time to think and gather my thoughts and realize that I had bigger and better things that I could be doing out there.

B.G. OF CASH MONEY MILLIONAIRES

I learned a long time ago that the best hustle is a legit hustle.

ICE-T

I used to be wild. It took me going to jail to realize, "Yo, let me just relax and slow down."

INSPECTAH DECK OF WU-TANG CLAN

No matter what anybody tells you, there is no glory in being locked up. Jail is for suckers, and I was one of them.

BLACK ROB

Jail ain't for real n*ggas. Real n*ggas stay on the street and make money.

PRODIGY OF MOBB DEEP

I just take it with pride that I have gotten through it and I have no felonies. But at the same time, the things I have been going through have shown me that life ain't easy.

LIL' ZANE

I can't afford to f*ck around. Life is too short and it's too much out here for me. Three strikes and you out. I ain't tryin' to see that.

CAPONE OF CAPONE-N-NOREAGA

There's nothing correct about the department of corrections at all. At the same time, nobody can rehabilitate anybody. You have to rehabilitate yourself.

NOREAGA OF CAPONE-N-NOREAGA

Violation is better than conversation. My time in jail helped me realize that I was either going to have a life of dealing drugs or a life of rapper.

SNOOP DOGG

Life ain't all about this thuggin', man. . . . I done served this time. I can't see myself walking back through those [prison] doors. That's not the life I want to live. Believe it.

DRAMA

I escaped prison; a lot of people ain't gonna be able to do that.

TRICK DADDY

You had the best clothes, the best cars, but you always ended up dead or in the pen. I said to myself, "I can't go to jail. I'm too fly for that."

ICE-T

Never thought life without you would be so rough . . .

LIL' KIM, "HOLD ON," *THE NOTORIOUS K.I.M.*

ON DEATH AND VIOLENCE 18

droppin' science

I'm just realizing that nothing protects you from the inevitable. If something's gonna happen, it's gonna happen.

THE NOTORIOUS B.I.G.

I don't have no fear of death. My only fear is coming back reincarnated.

TUPAC SHAKUR

I was used to gang-banging in Compton, so I just took it to the record business. But now that gang shit is dead. There ain't no roses blooming out of that negativity, man. And people don't want to hear it now, anyway.

DJ QUIK

American culture is hypocritical. We can't even point our finger like we pointing a gun in our video, but they can show guns on TV with no problem.

HAVOC OF MOBB DEEP

Everybody wanna see peace. I get tired of turning on the news and seeing motherf*ckers kill each other over and petty sh*t. I got hope that things will turn around.

KRAYZIE BONE OF BONE THUGS-N-HARMONY

When you're young, you think you're immortal. [My stroke] just showed me how mortal I really was.

JOE B'LAMO OF KOMPOZUR

It's tragic what happened to [The Notorious B.I.G.] and Tupac. But we have to survive.

NAS

We're not promoting violence, society's violent! That sh*t is really happening.

HAVOC OF MOBB DEEP

They killing over some stupid sh*t now. Over stupid reasons—over a b*tch that's just giving booty to everybody, over an argument, over money. You don't kill nobody over that.

DMX

Losing my sister in '94, that changed my whole perspective.

MYSTIKAL

You can have all the laws in the world, but you can't change people's hearts. The fact is that we're still dying; we're still being murdered. So we have to go into our communities and deal with each other. . . . We have to look out for our own.

TALIB KWELI OF BLACK STAR

Destroy these devils within your body and your soul and you will have no other choice but to go the right path. Stop killing each other, black on black, black on Latino; we gotta come together with love.

GHOSTFACE KILLAH OF WU-TANG CLAN

I don't think dying is sexy. I wanna see tomorrow. I wanna see my n*ggas with gray hair getting mad old. I wanna see all that sh*t. I've got a family to be there for.

BILLY DANZENIE OF M.O.P.

If you're out there wildin' with no meaning behind it, you deserve to get locked up; you deserve to get killed; you deserve bad luck.

PRODIGY OF MOBB DEEP

Violence is what you think is the remedy for stress, anger, defeat . . . there are better ways to deal with a f*cked-up situation. My solutions or recommendations are to 1) turn away from it, or 2) deal with the situation maturely by talking through your differences.

CAPONE OF CAPONE-N-NOREAGA

The sword is death. The book of life is peace.

WYCLEF JEAN

Sometimes you just have to walk away from something . . .

ICE CUBE

Bring your ones, not your guns.

METHOD MAN OF WU-TANG CLAN

There's a real problem with the youth and a real self-destructive mission that we're on. If we don't do something, it's going to get worse. I ain't no punk, but I believe that we could live peacefully. . . . I pray for a time when we are able to be proud of one another's achievements and not jealous.

GURU OF GANG STARR

I got shot under my eye in '91. . . . That was one of the worst things that happened to me.

MR. MARCELO

When those bullets eject, it's like saying, "So be it."

METHOD MAN OF WU-TANG CLAN

Anger has been a big part of my life. I've kinda snapped at times. When that happens, anything can trigger it. And before I know it, a whole lot of damage done. And for what?

FLESH-N-BONE OF BONE THUGS-N-HARMONY

[L]osing my dad to a drug overdose two years ago taught me the hardest lesson in life. Tell the people around you that you love them, because that could be the last time you ever see them.

MYSTIC

Dying is a doorway. And you don't die in a doorway. You go someplace else.

PHARELL WILLIAMS OF THE NEPTUNES

Violence is something that's never going to go away, whether it's in entertainment, in sports, or everyday life. But that doesn't mean you have to help enhance it.

DJ RED ALERT

You don't need no burner, man. You don't need to end up in the position I end[ed] up in. Go the other way, man. It ain't worth having your mother up in there broken up.

SHYNE

Now if you real, keep it real,
But if you fake, then you phony . . .

**504 BOYZ, "IF YOU REAL,
KEEP IT REAL," *GOODFELLAS***

ON KEEPIN'
IT REAL 19

droppin' science

The whole thing about being real is, it all just boils down to being honest. A lot of times adversity makes us overthink a situation and makes things more complicated than they really have to be. Being real is breaking things down to the bare bones of any given problem, not letting your pride or your emotions make decisions for you. We all know right from wrong; and that little reality check you give yourself before you deal with problems will then help you make right decisions.

SAUKRATES

Don't look at the label on the back of your shirt or on your behind to figure out who you are. Look at yourself in the mirror every day and make sure that what you see is what you can live with.

XZIBIT

If it makes you feel right, do it. Do what personalizes you.

DRE OF OUTKAST

There's a lot more to reality besides the ghetto and how f*cked up it is, and how much drugs you could sell.

SUPERNATURAL

I can't pretend to be, do, or be something I'm not.

LL COOL J

I say be proud of where you came from and represent.

EMINEM

I wouldn't be here if it wasn't for my mistakes.

COMMON

You gotta remember your roots, you gotta remember what got you where you're at.

INSPECTAH DECK OF WU-TANG CLAN

The people that's real with you, they're gonna be around you in hard times. People that ain't real, they're only gonna be around you in good times.

MASTER P, CEO OF NO LIMIT RECORDS

As long as I know who I am, all the other stuff is irrelevant.

DMX

Don't let none of the stuff go to your head. Don't ever act like you're too good for anybody . . .

LIL' BOW WOW

I'm honest. I give it to you how I feel it's to be told. I'm a realist. I deal with reality.

JA RULE

If a muthaf*cka got to make up a complete lie, and that sh*t sell a million records and he handled his business, taking care of his kids and his family— that's keeping it real to me. You ain't a real man if you can't take care of yourself.

THE NOTORIOUS B.I.G.

droppin' science

It's all about doing what's meaningful, eventually; like KRS-One said, "Respect will outlast cash."

GURU OF GANG STARR

The freedom to say and do what I want to do is my right, and I exercise that to the fullest.

BIG GIPP OF GOODIE MOB

You gotta deal with yourself.

BAHAMADIA

You gotta be real to yourself.

NAS

N*ggas gotta step up and take no sh*t. I ain't ever been afraid to put my balls on the table.

YOUNG ZEE OF THE OUTSIDAZ

It's not hard to be yourself. A lot of jail time helped me figure that out.

BLACK ROB

You gotta know the power of your words, and I think a lot of people neglect the power of their words.

ORACLE OF THE MASTERMINDS
(April 16, 2000. *Rebirth* magazine: www.rebirthmag.com)

No matter how much loot I get, I'm staying in the projects forever. That's our roots. That's what made us. Just like that saying, "You could take a n*gga out of the 'hood, but you can't take the 'hood out the n*gga."

HAVOC OF MOBB DEEP

Maintain your sense of purpose. Listen to yourself and know what you like.

GIFT OF GAB OF BLACKALICIOUS

I'm real with mine. That I'm 100 percent true to me. Once you find out how true you are to yourself, all this other sh*t in the world is yours.

RICHIE RICH

[I]t's just about being humble. If you ain't humble, sh*t will come back on you.

ZAAKIR OF JURASSIC 5

It's about keeping it real by being true to who you are and where you come from and knowing that being hard isn't as important as being yourself. And being yourself means never taking crap from other people.

JOHN FORTÉ

My motto is not to tell too much of your business, or at least not all of your business, because people might take it and do what they want with it. That's what my father says.

SOLÉ

Don't let yourself get wrapped up in anything that's not organic, I would say. And even some of the organic things, make sure you stay balanced and temper everything.

RAKAA-IRISCIENCE OF DILATED PEOPLES
(March 2000. *Rebirth* magazine: www.rebirthmag.com)

droppin' science

Don't be concerned with your last image; worry about your new one.

SIR MIX-A-LOT

My definition of keepin' it real is feedin' my family. Period.

TREACH OF NAUGHTY BY NATURE

Loyalty is what's missing from this game right now. I miss n*ggas with loyalty. I miss sharing. Now no matter what you're doin', you don't know who really loves you, and that's, like, the worst part of this business.

MASE

Ain't nothing changed. You'll still find me around the way with my peoples.

JA RULE

N*ggas don't know how it feels to sign an autograph with nothing in your pocket.

FREDRO STARR

You know, sometimes you don't know who to trust. Everybody tells you, "You can't trust nobody," but you gotta trust somebody, right?

MR. CHEEKS OF THE LOST BOYZ

You can do something to someone, but you better prepare for the repercussions. That sh*t comes from experience.

NAS

My people is everybody, not just black people. My people are people who enjoy what I do. My mama taught us to love and respect people who respect themselves, and that's how I bring it. That's just my character.

SNOOP DOGG

[B]ut I go through the same things everybody else does. I gotta pay taxes just like everybody else.

MISSY "MISDEMEANOR" ELLIOTT

A thing I have discovered from the success and some of [my] failures is that life is balance, and because you are striving for righteousness doesn't mean that you can't go out and kick it. Everything has two sides to it.

COMMON

I put myself in everybody else's shoes.

LIL' WAYNE OF CASH MONEY MILLIONAIRES

Just take the chance to know the person before you judge the person, that goes with anybody, not just me.

THE NOTORIOUS B.I.G.

You have to know the game you're in, know what you playing with, and know the rules.

SNOOP DOGG

When you runnin' a marathon, sometimes you take the lead, sometimes you stay back in the pack and you observe what's goin' on. If you always try to run in front the whole time, you gonna lose the marathon. I don't have a problem runnin' with the pack. You ain't gotta shine all the time.

SEAN "P. DIDDY" COMBS

droppin' science

Before I got a chance to get out there and really blow up, the accident happened. But everything happens for a reason. I got a chance to live my dream, so I'm grateful for that.

THE D.O.C.

Everybody can relate to pain. Everybody feels pain. I like to [rap about] pain.

TRAGEDY KHADAFI

Don't ever make yourself responsible for what other people do.

ERYKAH BADU

In the next millennium, kids is gonna be badder 'cause we ain't teaching them sh*t. We say children are the future. We got nothing but war going on. The Prez cheated. What are we teaching them?

METHOD MAN OF WU-TANG CLAN

You forget where you come from, and someone's going to remind you.

DMX

People be switching up, they start doing what everybody else is doing at the time. I feel like if you just put down what's in your heart, you stay real no matter what. Develop your own mind. Then if it's real from your heart, it's gonna happen for you no matter where you're from, no matter where you at.

YOUNG BLEED

I'm not Super Suzy Sunshine. But it's my duty to teach as I go along, say some things that are positive. It's what you have to do.

EVE

The feelings you let out, those are the best ones. It's like cryin' and sh*t. When you drop that tear, after you finish, you feel a lot better [than] from holding all that sh*t in. But a lot of people feel real ashamed, worried about how other people might think. But I learned to just go ahead. I don't give a f*ck what nobody says. If it's real and that's what it is, then that's what it is.

GHOSTFACE KILLAH OF WU-TANG CLAN

I'm living and learning every day. I'm good and I'm bad. I'm just a real person.

SEAN "P. DIDDY" COMBS

You can perpetrate whatever kinda fraud you want on TV or in magazines, but the people in the street, you can't hide from them. People gonna see what the real is, the word is gonna get out. So you might as well be real with people.

BUN B (AKA U.G.K.)

I've done everything you will ever do. And I've probably made every mistake you will ever make. You've got nothing to prove to nobody. But you gotta ask yourself what you want.

JAY-Z

Hate don't count. Hate means nothing.

TRICK DADDY

But I'm a f*ckin' human being. And I'm Marshall Mathers before I'm anything. Just a regular m*thaf*cker that stands up for what he believes in.

EMINEM

I know if my business is not straight, then my life is not straight. And that consists of making sure you pay the taxes, making sure you have a place to rest your head, and making sure you're taking care of the people around you, in your inner circle. Business is the first part, because . . . if you got too many bills, if you stressed out, then you can't create.

PARRISH SMITH OF EPMD

Being real means you won't jeopardize who you are as a person for whatever trend is popular.

FREDDIE FOXXX

But for younger kids . . . keeping it real means "Yo, if I hold a gun and I can shoot somebody, that means I'm brave and I don't give a f*ck about nobody," and that's distorted, that's *not* keeping it real . . .

POSDNOUS OF DE LA SOUL

When you start doing sh*t that doesn't feel like it was you, even if it could be kinda all right, people don't believe in it.

BUSTA RHYMES

I think . . . we get so caught up in wanting to keep it real, but in a business sense, you really can't get nowhere being like that.

MISSY "MISDEMEANOR" ELLIOTT

I don't want to be like anybody. I just want to be like myself.

LIL' BOW WOW

Women have weaknesses, but it's cool to show their strengths, too. And I show male strength by showing our weakness, because if we know we're weak, we can become strong.

COMMON

Getting old is just some sh*t you can't avoid. As long as you live, you're going to get old. You just gotta deal with it.

SCARFACE

I accept the things that I thought were so ugly and not right. I accept the way I speak. I accept not finishing high school. I accept a lot.

MARY J. BLIGE

People walk up to us and say stuff like "You all so down-to-earth." Well, that['s] the way we were raised. We say thank you for even the smallest thing. I mean, my grandma would look at me like I'm crazy if I didn't.

NELLY

Sometimes you've got to come out of an environment and sit yourself down and think about what you really want to do. Because life is real and you can die out here. A lot of people think it's cool, man, but the street life is not the life for a person—for anybody. White, black . . . you can die. And once you dead, you ain't got nothing.

PROJECT PAT

Keeping it real means keeping it real for myself.

MISSY "MISDEMEANOR" ELLIOTT

You can't never get too big.

JADAKISS OF THE LOX

droppin' science

Positivity and peace is not a bus stop you get off at. You gon' have to work on it every day for the rest of your life. 'Cause the crap seeps in. I don't care how grounded you are—it seeps in.

JILL SCOTT

Just say what you got to say in one ball and keep it moving.

PETE ROCK

I don't listen to radio or watch TV much; I'm not in a state of mimic, you know what I'm saying?

MISSY "MISDEMEANOR" ELLIOTT

How you gon' win when you ain't right within . . .

LAURYN HILL, "DOO WOP (THAT THING),"
THE MISEDUCATION OF LAURYN HILL

YA HEARD? 20

droppin' science

I don't care how small my world is . . . I am going to make it the best I can.
MASTER P, CEO OF NO LIMIT RECORDS

Everything's a blessing. . . . Sometimes when you lose, you really win.

AZ

If you can believe you can or if you believe you can't, either way, you're right.
JELLEESTONE

Money helps with happiness, but it doesn't help with joy. True joy comes from knowing one's own strengths. Strength comes through skill, skill comes through knowledge, and knowledge comes through practice.

KRS-ONE

Contrary to popular belief, common sense does not exist. You either have sense or non-sense. Sense is not common.

CHUCK D

Everything in life happens for a reason, and I accept that and don't question it.
SHYNE

People tend to take youth for granted. I mean, live your life to the fullest, but don't take it for granted.

ENCORE

There's always a flip side, and I tend to look at that before I pass judgment on anybody.

EMINEM

Respect other people and be responsible for your actions.

DARRYL "D.M.C." MCDANIELS OF RUN-D.M.C.

I know that I'm not perfect, but as long as I believe in God and myself, everything will be all right.

LL COOL J

Whatever you achieve, future, present, or past, never forget the ones who helped your ass!

LORD G

I'm a firm believer in thriving off the positive energy that's around you, and maintaining that level in order to get results.

BUSTA RHYMES

There's a time to be angry and there's a time to be peaceful.

COMMON

I don't care if I'm singing with TLC and we're selling twenty million records and tomorrow I'm sitting in a jail cell. Either way, I can live in that situation. It's not that I would prefer the jail cell over TLC, but hey, it's not gonna break me.

LISA "LEFT EYE" LOPES OF TLC

droppin' science

I believe if you think about something enough, it will come to pass. It's energy. Every thought you have, even though no one may hear it, it's going to become a reality.

DJ QUIK

To live is to suffer, but to survive is to find meaning in the suffering, and I'm gonna survive.

DMX

The revolution must first start with each individual changing [his or her] mind-set to one of understanding. Like existing in this world without just relying on materialistic things; not just relying on sex and alcohol and drugs. But letting your foundation be the Supreme Being. That's revolution.

COMMON

You know, freedom is all in the mind. If your mind is free, then you will always be free.

SHYNE

Truth doesn't change; only lies do.

BUSTA RHYMES

You don't get a second chance. One wrong move on the streets, and you're dead.

CED

Maintain your sense of purpose. Listen to yourself and know what you like.

GIFT OF GAB OF BLACKALICIOUS

I just want to be remembered as someone that was always in tune with his culture and his people. 'Cause you gotta know where you came from to know where you're going.

DJ TONY TOUCH

If Mama ain't tell me nothin' else, it was do something. No matter what you do, do it and be good at it.

PONNEE

Knowledge of one's identity, one's self, community, nation, religion, and God is the true meaning of resurrection, while ignorance of it signifies hell.

THE HONORABLE ELIJAH MUHAMMAD

It's knowing who we are that makes us strong.

CEE-LO OF GOODIE MOB

Keep your eye on the prize.

OL' DIRTY BASTARD OF WU-TANG CLAN

Know that you gotta do what you gotta do. . . . This is your life.

DRAG-ON

I don't regret nothing I did.

EVE

droppin' science

Time heals all wounds.

LAYZIE BONE OF BONE THUGS-N-HARMONY

Ain't nuthin' like havin' a life. When you get up in the mornin', you get another chance, another opportunity.

MASTER P, CEO OF NO LIMIT RECORDS

Hip hop is about good music and about strong lyrical content . . . I think it's very powerful because it's not the same ol' sh*t. We strive to educate, and we make good music. All the elements that are involved in hip hop, we have.

GRAND PUBA OF BRAND NUBIAN

You'll never be a leader if you're a follower. I know I'm a leader.

SWIZZ BEATZ OF RUFF RYDERS

I'm tired of being categorized as a gangsta rapper or just a rapper. I'm a businessman, and I want to be respected and viewed as a businessman.

MASTER P, CEO OF NO LIMIT RECORDS

There's about to be another world war, and it might become World War III. So if you're gonna get a deal, get it now. And make sure you get your advance.

RYU OF STYLES OF BEYOND

We are not on some old-school mission. We're not on an underground mission. We're just a hip hop group that does hip hop music.

Q-UNIQUE OF ARSONISTS

If you fix your mind on what you want to do and say to yourself, "I ain't gon' stop till I get it done," you will be the best. That's my motto: stick with it until it's done.

BAREDA

There are three things you don't change. You don't change mechanics, doctors, or beauticians.

MJG

Self-motivation is the best motivation. Self-employment is the best employment. And self-respect is the best respect.

LUDACRIS

That's what life is about. Just doin' it.

[DAVE] "TRUGOY THE DOVE" OF DE LA SOUL

[W]e need to stop makin' excuses. We shouldn't bitch, let's stand tall through it all. Till it come back around, we gotta continue to do our job. Whether it be up or down, roll with it, or don't f*ck with it at all. Feel me?

E-40

You gotta remember, everybody goes through cycles. You got good times. You got bad times . . .

GHOSTFACE KILLAH OF WU-TANG CLAN

Our words mean something, because we believe they can bring about change.

M-1 OF DEAD PREZ

Life is what you make it.

DA BRAT

droppin' science

Be original.

BLACK THOUGHT OF THE ROOTS

I'm not perfect. I'm human. I've made a lot of mistakes and there's a lot of things that I don't know, but I'm not afraid to learn, and not afraid to say that I don't know something.

FOXY BROWN

We have a voice for a reason, and I feel like we should use it. We don't all have to be Suzy Sunshine, but if you're gonna speak, then teach.

EVE

In order for individuals to work together, you gonna hafta compromise.

MYSTIKAL

Everything has a time and place.

SCARFACE

Friendship, respect, and loyalty are the top three things in my life.

DJ MUGGS OF SOUL ASSASSINS/CYPRESS HILL

Steel sharpens steel. Wood can't sharpen steel.

BEANIE SIGEL

[If] you keep your mind open and [don't] get trapped, you'll notice that everybody's just like everybody else.

MACK 10

I have a guideline to my life, and I just try to do the best thing for my life—not my mom's, not my father's—and that's going to make me happy when I wake up the next day.

MYA

My definition of womanhood is being and celebrating who I am.

EVE

Strap up. [Wear a condom.]

NELLY

Life is a struggle, but I wouldn't want it any other way.

MYSONNE

One of the secrets to longevity is that whatever you want to be long in, don't let it be the thing that's feeding you.

KRS-ONE

Now, if your enemy knows your weakness, he got an advantage over you.

FIEND

Stay in school.

CAPPADONNA OF WU-TANG CLAN

droppin' science

[I]t is only when you share with others that you truly begin to find the meaning of life.

DMX

My life is an expression of things.

Q-TIP

Patience is a *must,* not a virtue. Without it, you help to create friction and turmoil. With it, you help to expedite the manifestation of your visions and dreams!

LORD G

I know that nothing is for free and everybody wants something. You don't get nothing for nothing. As long as you keep it on that page, then you'll be all right.

SHYHEIM

Style ain't for sale, and you can't buy class with any amount of cash.

VANYLLA CHILE

Always be yourself.

SILKK THE SHOCKER

Be who you want to be.

LUTHER "LUKE" CAMPBELL

Be yourself and the world will love you.

FIEND

There is no substitution for happiness. Period.

SUGE KNIGHT, CEO OF DEATH ROW RECORDS

Just be yourself and know that you and your family come first.

LIL' ZANE

Work hard, and don't give up at what you really want.

MC EIHT

Wait to have kids.

MC LYTE

There are twenty-four hours in a day: twelve to mind your own and twelve to leave others alone.

SOLÉ

Nothing lasts forever. You can't take anything for granted.

BLACK THOUGHT OF THE ROOTS

Maintain your focus.

KRS-ONE

Pride will get your ass whooped and it will keep you broke.

MF GRIMM

Make sure you always put on clean drawers.

GHOSTFACE KILLAH OF WU-TANG CLAN

If you see it, take it, but make it your own.

DJ MUGGS QUOTING B.B. KING

We learned that you can't please everybody, so it's best just to please yourself first, and everything else will fall into place.

J-LAI OF PROFYLE

Don't ever give up; always set your goals and do whatever you can to try to achieve them.

GILLIE DA KID OF MAJOR FIGGAS

If you don't have your business straight, it's not going to last. And the number-one person to take care of your business is you.

LUDACRIS

Everything we do, we try to think, think about the effect of it today and tomorrow.

I SELF DIVINE OF MICRANOTS

Knowledge and understanding is the same.

RZA OF WU-TANG CLAN

God sends us here with exactly what we need, the perfect height, the perfect-looking face, the perfect voice, the perfect everything to accomplish whatever it is you're here for.

INDIA ARIE

The understanding that the truth gives you, and the freedom that the truth gives your heart, is something I think [why] man is capable of having and entitled to have.

RZA OF WU-TANG CLAN

A lotta times you don't control your own destiny, but you lead your own path into where you're going.

NOREAGA OF CAPONE-N-NOREAGA

[W]hen you're shining, you're the light.

EVIDENCE OF DILATED PEOPLES

No te rindas. Translation: Don't give up.

A SPANISH SAYING

So stay out of trouble, and that
    goes for me too,
That's what we need to do, that's
    my advice to you.

GURU, "MY ADVICE 2 YOU,"
MOMENT OF TRUTH

ACKNOWLEDGMENTS

No artist works in a vacuum. There are forces both seen and unseen that exist to touch you and bless you and help you move forward. There have been many who have shored me up as I've walked this journey to the here and now. And it's true: the journey is the reward.

God is so good. I thank you, God, for answering my prayers . . . I know the best is yet to come. Thank you, Carole Hall, for planting the seed in the first place. Thank you, Mannie Barron, for going to the well on my behalf, *twice*. Your vision for and faith in this book is something I shall cherish for the rest of my life. To my "team" at Random House: Rachel Kahan, my enormously helpful, always positive, wise-beyond-her-years "sistah-friend" editor; I thank you for taking me on and standing by me through this process. You've added new meaning to the word "loyalty." And Elizabeth Herr—who, through the entire permissions process, worked tirelessly and seemingly at the speed of light—I hope you know that you are very much appreciated.

Thank you, Elly Sidel, my agent *extraordinaire,* who saw it and claimed it for me even before I did. Linda Kirland, thank you for your love and friendship and, more important, for reminding me who I really am! Andy Bonime, thank you for your wisdom and innate intelligence. You're one of the smartest men I've ever met . . . God bless you!

Ms. DuBois: you've got the faith to move mountains, and I thank you for breaking off pieces of it and sharing them with me when I couldn't see. Yana, thank you for providing me with that wonderful safe space. You are most clearly a lover of my soul. Karen Lee, you are simply one of "da best," and I thank you for being a *Force for Good*! Donna Marie Carolan and William Rodney Foster—you fed me body and soul when I needed it the most; I love how you love me! Vinny Carolan Foster, thank you for showing me what joy truly is and for being a living demonstration of innocence. Please know that you are an immense blessing in my life! To Maia and your loving parents, Chuy and Maria, know that I value your friendship, honesty, and assistance—you truly have no idea how much they mean to me. Sharon Heyward and Lesley Pitts, your friendship is priceless—you remembered and, more important, you *acted* . . . who could ask for anything more? To my "kids"—C "Breeze" and LaLita Haynes and Adell O'Bryant—I hope you know you are all gems in my crown! My brother, Donald Lester McIver, I love you and miss you more than you'll ever know, and I thank you for being the first person to help me understand that, yes, Art *is* important!

Last, I thank my parents—Eulla Belle Howell McIver and Donald Henry McIver. Mommy, I thank you for instilling within me a love for the written word, and Daddy, thank you for teaching me to love learning. Your words of wisdom and the life lessons you've imparted will continue to serve me well.

Denise L. McIver has an extensive background in entertainment. In the course of her professional life, she has worked for CBS Entertainment, where she assisted in the development of new programming for its movies-of-the-week and miniseries department; was a production assistant for *The Fresh Prince of Bel-Air* during its third NBC season; and served as manager of media relations for Perspective/A&M Records. She is now a freelance media relations consultant for Warner Bros. Records, whose roster includes both Hip Hop and R&B artists. However, writing has always been her first love, and her passion led her to study fiction writing under the tutelage of PEN Lifetime Achievement winner John Rechy and with Jim Krusoe, editor of *The Santa Monica College Review*. Her published articles, which cover popular music and books, have appeared in *Africana.com*, *VIBE*, *Book*, Launch.com, *Daily Variety*, the *Los Angeles Reader*, *Black Beat*, and *Upscale*.

She resides in Los Angeles and is working on an untitled collection of short stories. *Droppin' Science: Straight-Up Talk from Hip Hop's Greatest Voices* is her first book.